TRUST KIDS!

Stories on Youth Autonomy
and Confronting Adult Supremacy

Edited by carla joy bergman
Foreword by Matt Hern

Trust Kids! Stories on Youth Autonomy and Confronting Adult Supremacy
© 2022 carla joy bergman
All essays © 2022 by their respective authors

This edition © 2022, AK Press (Chico and Edinburgh)

ISBN: 978-1-84935-385-4
E-ISBN: 978-1-84935-386-1
Library of Congress Control Number: 2022936905

AK Press   AK Press
370 Ryan Ave. #100   33 Tower St.
Chico, CA 95973   Edinburgh EH6 7BN
USA   Scotland
www.akpress.org   www.akuk.com
akpress@akpress.org   akuk@akpress.org

The above addresses would be delighted to provide you with the latest AK Press distribution catalog, which features books, pamphlets, zines, and stylish apparel published and/or distributed by AK Press. Alternatively, visit our websites for the complete catalog, latest news, and secure ordering.

Cover design by Siana Sonoquie
Cover mural by Mona Caron (https://monacaron.com)
Interior design by Casandra Johns
Printed in the United States

In Memory of Gustavo Esteva

The child in each of us
Knows paradise.
Paradise is home.
Home as it was
Or home as it should have been.

Paradise is one's own place,
One's own people,
One's own world,
Knowing and known,
Perhaps even
Loving and loved.

Yet every child
Is cast from paradise—
Into growth and destruction,
Into solitude and new community,
Into vast, ongoing
Change.

—Octavia E. Butler, *Parable of the Talents*

Contents

Artwork

Foreword

By Matt Hern

I was flattered to be asked to write the foreword to this fine collection. It's a sweet and thoughtful book written by people coming from an impressive array of directions. It's a powerful polemical demand: that we *trust kids*.

But I also feel a little awkward, a little fraudulent in agreeing to write this.

My own children have grown old, and while I still hang out with teenagers every day, I rarely get the chance to be with young kids anymore. So frankly, I feel a little unsteady on this ground.

Nevertheless, out of respect for all carla's organizing work and activism, and in the spirit of friendship, I agreed.

My first thought was: did I trust my own kids when they were young? I think so, generally, but not all the time for sure, strictly speaking. I trusted that they would lie to me on occasion, more so when they were teens: it would have felt weird if they didn't. I believed (and still believe) in their instincts, their good hearts, their brains, their hard work, their love.

But did I *trust* them? To do what? Learn basic hygiene? Make good choices? Go to college? Not sleep with Republicans?

Then I started thinking about the kids I have hung out with over the years. And the young people I spend my days with now. Do I really trust them? And what would that look like if I did? All of the families I hang out with come from different cultural, social, and religious backgrounds than I do, and everyone has different perspectives on parenting and family life. Who am I to tell anyone how to parent their kids, or to prescribe a good childhood, or to describe what *trust* looks like? The idea of trust is highly unstable, malleable, and permeable: it looks very different through different eyes.

And then I started thinking about why. *Why* should we trust kids? Why is that an imperative worthy of so much thoughtful writing? Who is not trusting kids now? And honestly, do I trust other adults? Should I?

I started floundering some.

But then I thought of a better question: why should anyone trust *me*?

I'm a settler living on unceded and occupied xʷməθkʷəy̓əm territory. My mongrel-Euro family has been living on Coast Salish territories for four generations now. I'm a middle-aged, middle-class cis-gendered white guy who spends all his days with racialized migrant kids on unceded traditional territories.

Which part of any of that biography suggests that *anyone* should trust me—kids or otherwise? Almost nothing of my identity or heritage suggests that I am a plausibly trustworthy person. How might I comport and conduct myself in a way that opens the possibility of being worthy of trust? It is a question that haunts white settlers, and one that I am far from sure how to answer, so I went looking in here for ideas.

I found many things in this book that gave me a lot to think about, and it was much more than just about trusting kids. That's some of it, but that demand is linked closely to larger questions of domination and exploitation. The writing I heard most poignantly was about building relationships everywhere that are defined by a substantive concern for the other—for humans as much as the other-than-humans: whether that is animals, trees, rivers, or mountains.

I heard that these relationships have to start at home; that familial and very personal relationships are so often ignored or relegated to inconsequential "lifestyle politics." The Left loves emancipatory social rhetoric but habitually fails to translate that to young people. The stakes are clear: if you want kids to learn how to live in a world full of domination, then start them early! If you want a world full of bosses, show 'em who's boss at home. If you want a world full of hierarchy, set your house up like that. If you want people living in fear and mistrust and suspicion, well, you know what that looks like.

What I heard instead were some sweet stories of older and younger people figuring out what trust might mean for them. I read about decolonizing parenting, and how family violence is so closely linked to white supremacy.

I read about how the historical arc of social justice traces gradual changes in the conceptualization and treatment of children.

I read about parenting as a relationship that isn't transactional, about how kids don't owe their parents anything.

I read that kids don't need to be taught joy in being alive. I read that we should "imagine honoring and respecting them as full and whole human beings, rather than deficient or less than, as weak and needing manipulation and control."

I read about making and remaking the world right here and now.

That's some of what I found here, and there is a whole lot more.

I really urge you to read this book. I don't know if you will find anything like what I did, but you will definitely find some beautiful, hopeful writing and a collection of powerful, challenging ideas.

Acknowledgments

I give my deepest gratitude to every single person out there who not only survived childhood but found ways to thrive—thank you for lighting the way. To all the weavers, storytellers, writers, and radical folks who have been resisting child oppression since it began, and who continue to, your words and actions are tangled up in mine throughout this book, thank you all. There are too many to name, but I am going to name a few and I am sure I am missing some here too, my apologies. Thank you Emma Goldman, Peter Kropotkin, Zach Bergman, Ivan Illich, bell hooks, Helen Hughes, Chris Mercogliano, Leanne Betasamosake Simpson, Zakiyya Ismail, Carol Black, Erik Fromm, Octavia E. Butler, and Ursula K. Le Guin.

As I was doing the final edits on this book, my number one mentor and dear friend, Gustavo Esteva passed away… It is with a deep sadness that I finish this book without him, and I am very grateful that he has a beautiful essay (co-written with his friends, Madhu and Dana) in the book. Gustavo's work and contribution lives on in all of us. Thank you, dear friend.

And, to John Holt—who the title *Trust Kids!* is a direct nod to—thank you for all the walls you unbuilt for and with kids, and for showing us adults the many possible pathways to better support and be in solidarity with young folks.

Thank you to my mentors, of all ages, who continue to live a thriving life while resisting. And big love to all the kids and adults that my family and I were and are privileged to co-learn alongside. We love you.

Thank you to AK Press for all the support and care along the way, including trusting that the book had to wait while we adjusted to the pandemic. I especially want to thank Zach Blue for loving the idea straight away, and thank you for promotional support and excitement, Christen Cioffi and Charles Weigl. Much appreciation to Lorna Vetters for doing a sensitive and beautiful edit of the manuscript.

To the wonderful writers and artists in the book, who together make this book what it is! I am forever grateful for all of your brilliance, care, and love: Noleca Radway, Dani Burlison and Enfys Craft, Uilliam Joy Bergman, Yasamin and Tim Holland, Idzie Desmarais, Akilah S. Richards, Meghan Carrico, chris time steele, Antonio Buehler, Sara Zacuto, Rebecca Solnit, Tasnim Nathoo, Jon Pawson, Maya Motoi, Wakaba, Joanna Motoi, Cindy White, kitty sipple, Chris Mercogliano, Lily Mercogliano Easton, Stacey Patton, Toby Rollo, Gustavo Esteva, Madhu S. Prakash, Dana L. Stuchul, Gabriel Zacuto, Zach Bergman, Chris Bergman, ck nosun, and Grant Hoskins aka Gadzooks Bazooka.

Many thanks to Matt Hern for writing the foreword! I am forever indebted to you for all your guidance and support over the years (in person and in your writing!). I am especially grateful for learning from you what it can look and feel like to truly show up for kids with curiosity, and more questions than answers.

I also want to give my thanks to the incredible folks who were unable to contribute to the book due to increased hardships caused by the Covid-19 pandemic. Your ideas and examples of living differently with kids are still in this book; I am grateful for our conversations.

And, wow, this cover! I am so grateful to Rebecca Solnit for connecting me to Mona Caron! And beyond grateful that Mona allowed me to use her fabulous piece, "Landing Pad" for the front cover image. It captured what I was trying to convey with this book in such a magical and inviting way. And I am grateful to Siana Sonoquie for working with that "Landing Pad" image to make this stunning cover—thank you both!

Thank you for reading the early manuscript: Tomas Moniz and Eli Meyerhoff.

Thank you to the wonderful writing collective, Curiousism Cyphers, whose poems provided me with so much joy throughout the process of weaving this book together.

Love and gratitude to all my friends and kin who are here and there and everywhere! Immense love to my friends for supporting my work on this book in subtle and direct ways—in particular: Jamie Leigh and Rook; kitty sipple; Lily, David, and their kiddos; Gustavo ; Mike Jo; Julie Flett; Maya Motoi; Tasnim Nathoo; Meghan Carrico; Melody Sherwood; Maria Taylor; Hari Alluri; Eleanor Goldfield; Marina Sitrin; Melissa Roach; and Rebecca Solnit.

Endless love to Nick Montgomery for helping with some editing and advice along the way. I am grateful for your ongoing friendship and for your generous and generative support; you've helped me to amplify my voice.

Much love and admiration to chris time steele for your endless generosity and support, for providing concrete guidance and excitement with and for the book, especially when I wanted to scrap it.

Forever love and gratitude to my sister, Candice Wright, who was first in having the courage to break toxic family patterns and show me another more loving way to be a mom.

Across all timelines and in all places, I give my deepest thanks and *all my love* to my partner and kids, Chris Bergman, Zach Bergman, and Uilliam (Liam) Joy! Having you three contribute your thoughts and ideas to this book was the best part for me. Truly. Thank you all for wanting to co-create here and everywhere, for mentoring me and co-learning with me on how to trust each other deeply, and you know the rest...

And lastly, because nothing is done in silo and we write to be read... To you—yes, you holding this book: thank you for reading this, and for perhaps picking up the wand to enact change.

Love,
carla

Introduction

By carla joy bergman

"If I had to make a general rule for living and working with children, it might be this: be wary of saying or doing anything to a child that you would not do to another adult, whose good opinion and affection you valued."
—John Holt, *Freedom and Beyond*

"Children need to be raised in loving environments.
Whenever domination is present love is lacking."
—bell hooks, *Feminism Is for Everybody*

"Kids are fully formed human beings the moment they come into this world. They know who they are, they know what they love, they know what to do! It is our job to be stewards of their humanness and provide the opportunities that they need to thrive. Not what you think they need to thrive, but what they tell you they need to thrive."
—Melody Sherwood (in conversation)

I

This is a book about relationships and love.
These are some of the stories; there are many more.
It's a book filled with curiosity, hope, and love.

Trust Kids! began with me thinking about how we can create *more* autonomous communities through deepening our relationships with children. And how, if we can shift these relationships, continue to bust open the patriarchal-nuclear family, create strong intergenerational connections, even in our radical communities, we may have a chance at long lasting change by co-creating a future that is local, decolonial, and autonomous, all amid the ongoing destruction of capitalism. I, and many others, feel these relationships across ages are vital to nurture and grow because, as long as there are seeds of hierarchy in our relationships, we will never fully escape our subjugation—those oppressive seeds will grow and spread, thwarting our collective capacity to be fully free.

I started using the phrase *Solidarity begins at home* because, as an activist and organizer I was seeing one of two things: that children and youth oppression is widely ignored or, alternatively, the conversation remains confined to schooling and school resistance. I could also say *Liberation begins at home,* or *Justice begins at home,* but those phrases lose a bit of what I am after here. At the heart of it, *Solidarity begins at home* is to be curious about, figure out, and affirm how adults who inhabit home and other public and private spaces with children and youth can have a concrete role in co-creating the conditions by which the children in their lives can enjoy justice and thrive. I truly believe that we must begin where we live, and start with our relationships—especially including the young folks—where power is palpable. If we can shift this power dynamic, truly undo ageism, including in our homes, the possibilities are endless for creating better worlds. I see these acts as solidarity.

I don't suggest that there's one path toward solidarity with children, in fact, part of trusting and listening to kids is being open to what the path forward can and will look like with them. Inclusion of kids also means that some kids may not want to be involved! Kids deserve the option, like all of us, to say *no.*

With this anthology, I was very interested in looking at and talking about the social borders between adults and youth, and also the ones between home life (whatever your configurations, but especially those beyond the nuclear family) and radical organizing life. In particular, I am interested in amplifying and affirming all the ways these borders and walls are continuingly being dismantled.

Youth oppression is still going strong

As much as I tend to write and engage in theory that is affirmative, sharing and amplifying these kinds of stories, I do wish that I didn't have to put this book together in 2021. I spent the summer of 2021 revisiting the works of the brilliant child and youth advocate John Holt (1923–1985) because he was committed to thinking about, writing about, and doing something about many of the themes in this book. In many of his letters to friends and colleagues, he was grappling with the treatment of kids, and aiming to get across how fundamentally vital it is to trust kids. And, while I am always inspired by his work, I also felt sad and a bit hopeless because, in all honesty, Holt was saying the same things, or fighting for the same things that many of us are still saying and fighting for today: *that kids and youth are already full humans and deserve to be treated as such.*

This is not to say that things haven't improved. Some things, such as the physical rights of a child and other examples of individual rights, have—especially in the public realm. These changes are the result of many decades of committed and fierce advocacy by activists and organizers, like Holt, who were working to break down the barriers young people face every day. You'll read some of these incredible examples and stories in this book, and perhaps you've experienced the changes yourself. Beyond the headlines and individual testimonies of youths who are being heard, there are still a devastating number of kids facing oppression in subtle or deadly ways, especially in their private lives. One only needs to look at the news to see that youth depression and suicide are on the rise.

Social change often comes in waves, and past movements and actions provide the necessary scaffolding for current generations to work off of—change is incremental and not one grand win. The all-ages work of carving out ways to thrive together amidst disasters, building friendships across differences, centering solidarity and generosity, and of course trusting kids, is not a straight line. It's an entangled tapestry of different voices, and it's beautiful. But there is still a lot of work to do.

Youth oppression is part of the machine that keeps the forces of Empire together. The deepening hold of capitalism on our everyday lives has made it more difficult than ever to imagine and enact social change and autonomy. Even when kids live in radical and supportive homes, they still face oppression and adult supremacy in their encounters with other adults. We've all been kids, and rather than collapsing us into sameness here, I'm instead highlighting this shared experience amid and within this uneven and unfair world. With this in mind, I suggest that, alongside a global movement for social transformation and change, the means and ends of organizing should be our everyday lives. To me, this means: solidarity begins at home, with the human and more-than-humans we depend on. From this perspective, this book is about amplifying stories and actions that reveal the liberatory potential in undoing the social borders that cut us off from each other and the world. This work attempts to amplify more stories about the neglected field of understanding and enacting social transformation.

Weaving past and current lineages

With a bit of hopelessness in my heart, I started thinking more about the curation of this anthology. I wanted to invite folks who haven't before been in the conversation about youth autonomy, or perhaps not in conversation with the other folks who've been writing about and working for youth autonomy for decades. I intentionally included folks who do not have kids of their own, or who haven't previously written about these ideas, because many of my mentors and some of the most incredible organizers and allies for liberation and youth autonomy over the years are adults who did not parent. My desire was to create ways to bring together these (newer) voices with those who have been in this conversation for a long time, and all the folks in between.

The scope and the structure of the book

At the heart of the book are conversations about the ways that children can be included, loved, and cared for in more generative and just ways. Essays explore the liberatory potential of consent, autonomy, love, and care, in relationships between children, youth, and the adults in their lives. Some essays trace where and how child oppression took root in our society and how it is part of the colonial, white supremacist system. Some essays more directly discuss adultism/adult supremacy (often called *childism* or *misopedy*), offering a critique of adult supremacy as a barrier to transformation and to children's thriving, showcasing how child oppression as it is lived today in many places isn't the "natural" way of being in kinship with the youngest members of our families and communities. There are essays that expose the violence and non-consensual interactions that kids face every day and explore the ways in which these patterns can continue into adulthood, reproducing child oppression in future generations.

While institutionalized oppression in schools, school resistance, and the alternatives of deschooling/unschooling are touched upon in some essays, school is not the central focus of this book. In this sense, *Trust Kids!* aims to disrupt the notions that school is central in children's lives, and that the oppression of children hinges on schooling. Instead, we take a step back and start at home, in our most private places. Because children can't live alone, power and privilege are necessarily at play there, no matter the configuration. So home is crucial to explore. Home can be the site of some of the most deeply rooted forms of oppression or it can be a place of safety.

Trust Kids! is also part inspiration, exploring, and amplifying other ways of being with our youngest (no matter what our role is in their lives), ways that are liberatory, decolonial, democratic, love-centered, and joyful.

As I arranged the different elements of the book, my intention was to create a flow between the pieces, weaving together many different voices and stories. My goal is not to erect borders and boundaries, but rather to create intersections. At each intersection in this layout there is a poem by the anonymous writing collective, Curiousism Cyphers. Here's what they say about the role of their poem: "*New Thorns* was inspired by themes and essays in *Trust Kids!*, as well as our own interests in the topic. Our hope is that our weaving poem can provide a way to pause and reflect—kind of like a beat, or perhaps be like a chorus in a song—and create a space for listening."[1]

So, there is a flow and it's something like this (although many of the threads run through the book): The first group of essays are from home, or relationships across ages that go beyond the home. The second group looks more at school, the alternatives to schooling and institutions, and school resistance, and includes a fictionalized piece. The third group shares essays and stories about breaking down the social borders between private and public life, while also weaving in themes and stories from the first two sections. The final group of essays focuses in on the historical and ongoing horrors that kids face, as well as some of the pathways toward youth autonomy. It's the more theoretical and historical part of the book, and it also aims to untangle the roots of childism/adult supremacy while highlighting ways of cultivating autonomy with kids all amid the ruins. And finally, an outro, titled "Back to the Beginning," which is poetic and to me, sums up the book.

What *Trust Kids!* is not

Trust Kids! is not a parenting handbook. It's not saying that parents suck, or that you suck. It's not showcasing the only people who have it figured out—though there are personal stories of beautiful everyday relationships with children that are inspiring for us all to read, and worth celebrating! One thing that's certain: there isn't one guiding ideology for this work, and not everyone in this book follows the same path toward youth autonomy and liberations. As such, then, this book doesn't provide a road map, but instead many different and creative paths toward trusting kids more.

On embracing different writing styles, and being a weaver instead of an editor

"Better to kill everything in their writing they DON'T love as much. Until only the darlings remain."—Brian K. Vaughan, *Saga*, Vol. 3

---

1   Curiousism Cyphers correspondence with carla bergman, December 2021.

I am very interested in amplifying different voices and writing styles, sharing voices not always heard, alongside more seasoned writers, and weaving them together in a beautiful tapestry (at least that's the goal!). I aim to break down barriers that often say who can and who cannot write, supporting neuro-differences (and neuro-fabulousness) along the way!

My aim with this "weaving" together is to show that resistance and autonomy is always in motion. I want to also amplify the words and actions happening today, but not erase all the work that came before.

II

"Real generosity towards the future lies in giving all to the present."—Albert Camus, *Notebooks 1935–1942*

In many ways, this book has been in the works for over twenty years, but I always hesitated writing about it in a direct way because, when adults write about youth oppression, especially us parents, we tend to center ourselves. It's a paradox. But, I believe that this collection of essays has done something different, thanks to all of the amazing contributors, and we welcome you, dear reader, to the conversation.

Trusting ourselves and each other is always a journey, never a destination. You will never reach a place of "perfect trust"... In fact, you are sure to keep messing up—trust me! You will fail; you will be human, you will (mis)use your power at times. We all do. Your kids, or kids in your life, may not trust you. The key, to me, is that we build a foundation of trust with kids, whereby the younger folks in our life can talk to us when they feel we are not trusting them well. If trust is flowing, it'll be powerful and beautiful. Then together, we can create borderless futures, ones grounded in love.

Rooting for Love

By Curiousism Cyphers

> "I come with empty hands and the desire to unbuild walls."
> –Ursula K. Le Guin, *The Dispossessed*

A seed can be a coffin or the beginnings of a home
The petals give hugs, sweet scents, no one pollinates alone
A seed bed where dreams are sowed
A deep thread where seams are sewed
When the hem is ripped out we'll see the borders were never real
We're childing the world from the power that adults wield
The trees gave us water while you taught us to sell it
But you are desert makers, scared of the world and selfish
Join us at the intersection where we all have been
And together we will share and decompose the queen
We will use our fractured selves and build a fertile home
From our collective dreams that were sewn with love,
Knitting bonds of familial ties that thrive beyond the bloodlines
Let us all remember our ancient borderless kin who composed songs beneath
    the rubble
Who gave our feet warmth as we struck and did good sabotage, that power
    renamed trouble
Their enduring whispers entangled with wind and water, and birds too, and If
    you are willing you can Hear their timeless and collective song in the beau-
    tiful wordless musings of infants and child
Interwoven stories of us, a tapestry of ageless kin folks
We each add a patch to the quilt, we begin to sew, solidarity begins at home

Out and Open

By Noleca Radway

When folks find out that I am a mother of three queer children, they often ask about how and when they *came out*. Now I know *coming out* is not a singular event, there is no before and after, no one moment, no one story. *Coming out* is non-linear and iterative, small and bold. *Coming out* happens in the in-between, when no one is looking but everyone is watching. *Coming out* is a constant becoming.

I did not know any of this when my middle child, Moxie, sat across from me at our small white circular kitchen table and said, "Mom, I think I might be gay."

I remember feeling this sense of closure, like the unknown was now known. At ten years old, Moxie had done it, defined themselves and now we could all get on with the business of being a queer family with a gay child.

Every single word of that sentence (mom, I, think, I, might, be, gay) rings in my ear like a dog whistle. I find myself constantly trying to decipher the deeper meaning, putting my english degree from Howard University to good use. "Mom" is a soft place. "I think I" is a metaphor for metacognition, that ability to think about one's thinking. "Might" communicates doubt and questioning. "Be Gay" is an oxymoron because "be" refers to (self) who you are and "gay" refers to (other) who you love.

Moxie's *coming out* led to many others in our tribe recognizing, exploring, and naming their own queerness. During a late night Internet search for language to support Moxie, I discovered the term demisexual, a sexual orientation where people only experience sexual attraction to folks that they have close emotional connections with. As I read more, I began to see myself, my queerness.

We were in it together, me and my three daughters, Black Queer women, fighting the patriarchy, calling out racism, and pushing back against hyper masculinity. There were many hard moments, like crying in the bathroom because we don't look like our barbie dolls or having our pants pulled down on the playground by a group of boys as part of their game or having none of the white kids in our class show up for our birthday party. Many hard moments, but we were on the same team and our team was the best and we all believed it.

At that time, one of the main tenets of my parenting philosophy was *prepare*, over *protect*. I didn't believe that I had the power to really protect my children from the world so instead I decided to look at the hard stuff and to prepare them for what was to come. But how do you prepare your child for the things you can't see coming?

At thirteen, Moxie *came out,* again.

I was away from home all day. As I turn my key and step over the threshold, I feel an ease in the air. As a mother of three, that is always a welcome surprise. Everyone is good, happy and content. I do all my transitioning inside rituals, take off my coat and shoes, wash my hands, take in each of my children. Within ten minutes, I am lying in my bed next to my partner catching up on our day. Moxie peaks through the door I left ajar.

"I have discovered something about myself that I want to share with you," Moxie says with a reserved excitement.

"Whenever you're ready, we're here," I respond.

I blink, and Moxie is spread out at the foot of my bed.

"I was thinking about it and I realized that I'm a boy." His voice is clear and steady.

We both respond with love and acceptance. Moxie sheds happy tears and tell us we are the best parents ever and then is off to play with his sisters.

Two years earlier, I went to a workshop where they gave out gender pronoun pins. By the time I arrived, all of the she/her and they/them pins were gone. For reasons only the ancestors and my spirit guides know, I picked up two he/him pins and put them in my pocket.

I suddenly remember exactly where the he/him pins are. I get up, retrieve them and hand them to Moxie. His face lights up. Moxie loves pins, he has pins all over his clothes, jackets, and things. Moxie coordinates his pins to match outfits and moods. When I ask Moxie about that moment he says "I felt seen and known."

I am so grateful that my children taught me to be scared, unsure, and still move toward love. Love keeps my internalized oppression at bay.

I didn't know what "I am a boy" meant for Moxie or for me.

For reasons I'm still unpacking and unlearning, including transphobia, I connected "I am a boy" with my girlfriends that identify as masculine centered rather than my students that identify as transgender.

Moxie came out to me again a few weeks later.

Moxie is part of an art collective. He is the youngest artist on the team, so I join the zoom meetings as support. As we sign in to the call, I type our names and pronouns: Noleca (she/they), Moxie (he/they). I remember feeling both nervous and proud. This was the first time I was introducing Moxie as *he*, I wanted to get it *right*. The facilitator asked everyone to introduce themselves and say their favorite tree. Moxie fidgeted as he sat next to me, distracted by our image on the computer screen. I click the Hide Self View tab and hold Moxie's hand in an attempt to ground us. I feel Moxie's body relax as we watch and listen to everyone introduce themselves. Then it's our turn.

"I'm Noleca, she/they, and my favorite tree is a cotton tree."

"I'm Moxie, he/him. My favorite tree is a willow tree."

When Moxie introduces himself, I feel something shake inside, like I am hearing this for the first time. Maybe it is the clarity in which he says he/him, maybe it is the way it stands in opposition to what I wrote.

Later that night, our family of five cuddled before bed. I lay next to Moxie on his loft bed and he turns to me.

"Mom, I want to tell you something. I know something for sure. I am not a they. I am a he."

Time stops. Suddenly I am looking at myself and have so many questions for Noleca.

1. WTF?
2. Did you know, and for how long?
3. Just how transphobic, sexist, homophobic, ageist, and racist are you that Moxie has to keep telling you the same thing over and over again?
4. Can you protect Moxie?
5. Can you prepare Moxie?
6. Are you part of the oppression that is keeping Moxie from affirming his gender?
7. Do you love yourself?
8. Why can't you let go of Moxie as she?

I feel the tears start to build up behind my eyes. I am triggered as fuck. I want to run and hide. My head talk is all judgment and self-hate.

I remember to take deep breaths.

Years before "I'm a boy" but after "I think I am gay," my therapist suggested I watch Brene Brown's TED Talk: "The Power of Vulnerability." Apparently the way I numb my feelings in order to hold space for people in my life and protect myself from emotional pain was cause for concern.

Who knew?

My children knew. Their bullshit meter is always on 10. While I was busy performing progressive educated pro-Black super mom, my children were ringing the alarm.

Blu would whisper, "I never know what you are thinking or feeling."

Moxie would ask, "Do you love me?"

Glory would scream, "You are the worst mother ever!"

I dismissed their words as childish insecurities that had nothing to do with me. It was the outside oppression of the world that was causing them to question their mother's love and intentions. I would gaslight them with words and actions, trying to convince them that they did not know what they knew. I weaponized the tools of the oppressor to maintain my own status quo.

In all fairness to myself, I believed my bullshit.

Most of the space in my childhood mind was occupied by thoughts of my mother. She was a force, everyone's favorite. To me, she was a goddess that controlled the moon, the sun, and stars. I wanted to be her, to protect her, to please her and to touch her. I studied her carefully. My mother shared her whole self with her children. When she was angry she yelled, when she was hurt she cried, when she was joyful she laughed, when she was confused she stumbled. As a child, I centered myself. I believed that I was the cause of all of it so I tried to morph myself to make my mother constantly happy. When it didn't work I blamed myself.

As an adult and educator I knew better, but the trauma was not healed. I thought my ability to shut off my feelings, squash my concerns, ignore my fears, and push forward would shield my children from me and all the rage, anger, and resentment that simmered right below the surface. I didn't want them to think that they were the cause of my pain.

Through therapy, meditation, and spirituality, I realized that by shielding Blu, Moxie, and Glory from my pain I was also shielding them from my love. So I stopped numbing myself and started practicing vulnerability. I knew my mother and she knew me. And although she rarely said it, I knew she loved me, all of me. I want my children to know me, all of me.

Breathing reminds me to have compassion for myself. I stay in the room, mind, body, and soul. I apologize for my hesitation.

"How do you know so much about who you are in this world?" I ask.

"The world is big and I look at it and I see all of it and then I pick the parts that work for me," he responds.

We talk about breasts, beards, penises, pregnancy, hormones, hips, vaginas, vulvas, feet, faces, hands, hips, swimsuits, and smiles.

We question if masculinity can exist without hyper-masculinity. We celebrated Black womanhood. We acknowledge the nuance of gender.

We talk, cry, and laugh together for hours. We all decided to figure this out together. We affirm that the goal is not to get it right. The goal is to love ourselves and each other through this transition.

The first time Moxie *came out* to me he was five years old. At that time I would often find Moxie talking to himself in the mirror. I would watch from afar wondering what magic was being manifested. One day he signaled me over. I remember feeling so special to be invited into his world.

"Mom, do I have a boy's voice?" Moxie asked, staring at himself in his favorite purple dress with the silver stars.

Without hesitation I responded, "You sound like Moxie to me."

His little face looked up at me, unsatisfied, but trusting.

He looked back at the mirror hoping to find the answer.

"I think I have a boy's voice," he replied earnestly.

I stood there silent, holding space.

I heard Moxie's question as an insecurity, instead of what it was: an affirmation!

I often wish for that moment back, hoping I would do better, be better.

But Moxie reminds me that it was enough to know that he was loved.

There are not a lot of pictures of Moxie smiling as a child, but he was happy. Maybe not *happy*, but alive, curious, open, sure. I saw him right away, because he was me. I took for granted the space between us, the ways we are different. The gap seemed so small, easy to stretch across whenever I was ready or needed to connect.

Now I mind the gap as I watch Moxie expand and bloom.

"Mom, you know that even if I was AMAB [Assigned Male At Birth] I would still be my mother's child," he graciously offers. "All of who you are is part of me that is greater than gender."

I am so grateful I was vulnerable in that moment so I could receive all that love.

"A Little More Rainbow: A Conversation About One Transgender Experience"

By Dani Burlison and Enfys Craft

I became a parent when my first child was born the week after my twenty-second birthday. As I raised my two kids as a single parent, I became deeply involved with social justice movements and included my children in much of my education, activism, and work in our community. I've also done my best to allow my children autonomy, particularly when it comes to their bodies and appearances: piercings, crazy hair, and eventually tattoos. I've always trusted their judgment and we've always communicated openly and honestly about our relationships with each other and our relationships with our own bodies. They've never had much to rebel against.

When my son came out as trans, it wasn't a surprise to me and I support him the best I can as he steps further into his bodily autonomy and finds ways to feel physically in alignment with who he is. As he continues growing into adulthood, I see that he is happier and more confident than he's ever been. This conversation took place when he was twenty-five and centers his experience with coming out, based on some of the questions other parents have had for me about his transition, and how our lifestyle as a family supported his self-exploration.

The name Enfys means "rainbow" in Welsh and fits his transmasculine nonbinary fabulous self like a custom-made crown.

Dani: When did you first know or realize that you were trans?

Enfys: It's a little complicated because I went back and forth for a really long time. The first time that I considered it seriously was probably in high school, when my friend came out as trans. I started questioning gender stuff a little bit more. I think I was a little overwhelmed with it, so I don't think that I really accepted it until you suggested I see a therapist when I was twenty-one or twenty-two, because I kept bringing it up. And I was like, okay, this is a thing I should probably deal with a little bit more.

Dani: What I remember is that you were playing around with gender fluidity. You would present certain genders pretty extra at different times. And then, sometimes, be a little more gender neutral. I feel like that started when you were probably thirteen. I noticed it when you were really young.

Enfys: Looking back, for sure. There was some stuff going on.

Dani: When you told me, did you feel relieved, or worried, or did you think I'd be surprised?

Enfys: Definitely relieved. I didn't think you were going to be surprised. But there are two parts to that. I was nervous about it. And also, up until recently, I've based a lot of what I did about my personal identity stuff on my concern with what other people thought about me. So the tiniest things I would over inflate in my head and internalize for a really long time. I'm just such a self-conscious person in general. I'm a lot more confident now. But forever, I've been the most self-conscious, freaked out little anxiety person because I was in the closet.

Dani: Do you think that you felt self-conscious because you're trans, or do you realize that everybody feels that way when they're teenagers?

Enfys: It's both. Because I think I'm just naturally a little bit more inclined toward that. And I think that anybody in the closet internalizes everything that you see out in society. It was just compounding on itself and a bunch of different things. Part two was a little bit more philosophical. Part of why I was so nervous about being trans was because we grew up with goddess spirituality and goddess tradition witchcraft stuff, and so much women's empowerment, which I think is really important. And I think if I had been a cis dude, that would have been important for me to learn anyway. I didn't know what a TERF [trans exclusionary radical feminist] was but I had some of that anxiety of like, "Oh, if I am not a woman, then I'm betraying women by abandoning my assigned gender," or "How am I going to be able to connect to this spirituality that I grew up with?" and then I got super uncomfortable with it. And that's why I stepped away from our spiritual community for a long time. And that's why, when I started working at [the local witchcraft store], things really started coming up for me because it was a spiritual workplace. It was retail, but also you're providing a spiritual space for people. And it's centered around goddess spirituality. So, it was just awkward, uncomfortable.

Dani: Did you think I was going to feel that way, or do you think people in our witchcraft community would feel that way?

Enfys: I think just people in general. It's definitely a thing that I see now that I know about TERFs, that they think things like: this "woman" couldn't handle misogyny and she felt like the only way she could escape was becoming a man. It's like, "No, he's a man." That kind of stuff. I didn't have the whole complex understanding of the TERF scheming stuff yet.

Dani: I'm glad you didn't yet, partly because that shit is toxic and fucking cuckoo pants. It's crazy.

Enfys: I think it would have taken me a lot longer if I knew about TERFs so young.

Dani: It makes me think about when you came out publicly on social media, and one relative told you that you were actually a lesbian.

Enfys: A confused lesbian. It's like, uh, plot twist, no. It was just dumb. I did like that I didn't have to acknowledge her or anything. Because a couple of your friends who are cis women, and I think several of them are straight cis women, were like "gender and sexuality are different!"

Dani: I'm curious, do you think about that rite of passage ceremony [for newly menstruating youth] that I made you go through before your transition at the women's herbal symposium? You seemed so into it.

Enfys: I was definitely so into it. But I did feel self-conscious and a little bit weird. But I think that's one of the things that, even outside of gender boundaries and stuff like that, we're missing in our Western societies a lot, is the rites of passage thing that a lot of cultures historically had. Which is why I wanted to do the second ritual around top surgery and finally picking a name that feels really good.

Dani: What are some things that I did right? Other parents that might be reading this: you have a kid that comes out as trans when they're a teenager, or you suspect they're going to, and you want to support them.

Enfys: One of the main things is that because you've been so involved with activism my whole life... Even if you didn't really know trans people, or weren't super aware of the issues, it wouldn't have taken you a lot to get caught up. And I think that's one of the main things that parents, even if you have a kid that you think is cis or whatever... You should take time to learn about gender issues regarding trans and non-binary people—some of whom aren't necessarily comfortable with the word *trans* for themselves. Because even if your kid ends up being cis and straight, the way Gen Z is right now, so many kids are able to come out so much earlier, so your kid is probably going to have a trans classmate or non-binary friends. Number one, follow people on social media, put it in your life where it's normalized if you don't have your own friends and stuff. Follow trans and non-binary people with different opinions so that you're not just like, "Oh, this is the model for all trans people." Also, even just having gender nonconforming people around.

You are also involved with alternative communities. And you're just a weirdo in general. So, I think that made things a lot more comfortable for me. Being around alternative community—meaning being involved with social justice and activism, or at least knowing about it from a young age—helped me. And knowing that you were involved with it. Being around weirdos, and being weird, or different or open minded. All of that just makes space for your kid to be different from the status quo.

Dani: So, exposing kids from a young age to a variety of different types of people, and communities, and things like that?

Enfys: Yeah, we never had cable in your house. Studio Ghibli, weird 80s fantasy movies like *Labyrinth*, and *Legend*, documentaries about all different types of people and places and issues, travel shows.

Dani: And that Crimethinc documentary about the WTO protests in Seattle, ha!

Enfys: One thing that I wish we did a lot sooner was to have an in-depth conversation like this. I don't think I was super ready for it right away, but it also felt like we just weren't talking about it a whole lot, which I know was probably just you trying to be chill and not make it like this weird big deal, not trying to stress me out.

Dani: Because it didn't feel like a weird big deal to me, because it was such a long unfolding process that when you finally said something, I was just like, "Yeah, we've been in this for a long time." The first time anything felt like a big deal, and it wasn't even that big of a deal, was when you wanted to start testosterone while you were still having health issues. And it wasn't about you starting hormones, I was worried about how it would impact your health. And I wanted you to make sure that was under control. We had so many smaller conversations over the years building up to the big come out, that it felt like we had already talked about it, most of it.

Do you think other families should have a more in-depth conversation early on?

Enfys: Not necessarily an in-depth conversation. Definitely, read up a little bit before having a big conversation with your kids, so that it's not all on them. But also having more bonding, putting everything more clearly on the table. Because you're right, we did talk about a lot, but it was all when I was really confused, and when my memory and all my health stuff was really still fucked up. So, I don't remember most of those.

Up until the last couple of years, my memory is so fucked up and not great, because I was dealing with the chronic illness, the dysphoria, and dissociation. I don't think we've ever really talked about how bad my dissociation was, but it was bad-bad. I don't have a lot of my memory from after puberty, honestly.

Dani: That makes sense that you don't remember a lot, and thought we should have had more of a conversation because I felt like we were having conversations ongoing. You've been gender nonconforming since you were thirteen. Watching you grow up, and as your parent, it was just an ongoing evolution. So for me, it didn't feel like, "Oh my God, all of a sudden this is a thing."

At the same time, it is a big deal, because of how the world is, safety issues around transphobia or not being seen for the gender you are in the world, and all of that stuff. But at home, it was so not a big deal.

Enfys: I think not having a sit down and talk, but sitting down and chatting about it more. And a note to parents: it's going to be different for each trans person and trans kid, what kind of tone they're comfortable with or want to have. So, just trying to follow the cues, or if you're having a hard time telling what they're comfortable with, because you're a little overwhelmed as a parent, just be upfront and be like, "If I'm being too overwhelming about this, just let me know, and I'll totally chill out. Or at least do my best." Because I know that's not easy for everybody.

Dani: I'm curious how the dysphoria and dissociation switched for you, or if it was helpful for you when you started testosterone, or was it therapy, or was it a combination? Was it getting back in touch with the witchcraft community? What helped the dysphoria and dissociation the most?

Enfys: What helped the most was getting specifically trans mental and physical health care. Well, mental health care first. Even having my therapist, until much more recently I was having this huge thing where I would get stuck in thinking loops really easily, and so I couldn't process and couldn't untangle all of my gender feelings without the help of an outside person who was used to doing that. Which I think is why I went back and forth so much, even with worrying about what other people would think and everything. And then, definitely, starting testosterone helped. Especially, because I remember when I was at my dad's, I was having a more difficult time getting my prescriptions filled, and I couldn't get them delivered—because they're highly controlled substances. And my hormones were inconsistent; I wasn't able to be on testosterone for a little bit. And it just extra fucked with my mental health on top of everything else that was going on when I was living there.

Dani: Other than that one friend of yours in high school, did you have other trans folks in your life? Or do you remember meeting some of my trans friends?

Enfys: I remember your trans friend in our neighborhood when I was little. And I feel like there were a couple of other trans women. But being younger, I don't remember knowing any trans men or trans masculine nonbinary people. So, until junior high school I thought you could literally only be transgender if you were a trans woman.

Dani: How do you feel about our community knowing? Have you felt supported by our friends and community?

Enfys: Everyone's mostly had really good etiquette around the whole thing. Because I don't talk about it that openly on social media, they've known not to be prying or anything like that. But don't think it's something we can't talk about. They'll say something like, "Hey, how's it going? You seem like you're feeling really good. Is it okay for me to ask how that is?" And I'm actually pretty open to talking about it one-on-one, in person. I was recently talking to someone about how I like normalizing it, and demystifying it, with casual conversation.

Dani: I'm curious about your thoughts about gender roles and how family members perceive them and get confused about what *nonbinary* or *trans masculine* and other terms mean.

Enfys: *Transmasculine nonbinary* is the term that fits me best, I think, at least from a technical standpoint.

Even if I were a binary gender, I would still be gender nonconforming. And that's actually a part of what helped me realize that I was more nonbinary after I transitioned. I felt a really similar pressure to present masculinely, to present as a certain type of guy, like when I was in the closet. When people treat me as a very specific kind of guy, I think it's because they want to be gender affirming.

Dani: That makes sense. So, they're trying to be self-aware, and show you acceptance and support, but then it's also reinforcing gender roles.

Enfys: It's a weird tricky spot because some trans people are really happy with a lot of that.

One of the weird things I miss is getting compliments on my physical appearance, which I actually struggled with a lot because I think it's just more socially acceptable and people are more comfortable complimenting feminine-presenting physical appearances, whether it be eyes, fashion, hair, hairstyle or hair color, jewelry, makeup, et cetera. Versus guys; girls don't like to compliment guys.

Dani: Girls don't want to talk to guys.

Enfys: Yes. But also, even if they're like, "Oh, I think that guy has really amazing eyelashes," or "I love his haircut," or "I think those are nice shoes." If they compliment … a lot of guys will interpret it as flirting, and as an invitation to flirt, and ask for a number, and stuff like that.

Dani: That's why we only compliment very obviously gay men because it's safe. And they fucking appreciate it.

Enfys: Yeah. And I think that's something that I actually struggled with at first. Most people started complimenting me less because of social gender roles and I was like, "Oh my God, am I ugly now, because I'm trans?" And as I started passing for more masculine in work situations, the amount of compliments that I got from strangers drastically reduced. This was at the movie theater. And also, at the witchcraft store. And I wonder how much of it was that for a long time, I was in a weird limbo spot, where I looked like a butch lesbian. I think because of that, women didn't want me to think that they were flirting with me. So, either way, if you're a guy, or you're perceived as queer in some other way, you get complimented less because people don't know how you're going to take it.

Dani: I compliment you!

Enfys: People are less inclined to believe compliments from their moms. That's just how it is.

Dani: So, last question. In the context of gender identity, what does the word *autonomy* mean to you, as a trans person?

Enfys: I think in the context of gender and being trans, autonomy is heavily connected to what we do or don't do with our bodies, because a lot of people don't want to, or don't care to, transition medically. Either because they're nonbinary and they're comfortable with their bodies, or even if they are binary, they don't have physical dysphoria.

It's so different for everybody. It's getting to do what we want with our bodies, how we want to do it, at the pace that—hopefully—we get to set without other people putting judgment on that, and still being respected.

Dani: One of the things you said: not everybody wants to have surgery, or take hormones. And I think that's part of that binary, people expect the gender role stuff, like you need to be really masculine or really feminine. And there's not a lot of mental space for that in some cis people's imagination. Is that accurate?

Enfys: Yeah. And I think if you're around someone, or close to someone, or have someone you really care about who's trans, or even gender nonconforming or nonbinary, creating space for them to essentially customize themselves. Because not everyone is going to create that space. And having that space within your inner circle makes a world of difference. I've seen so much stuff about younger trans guys coming out and feeling pressure to do things in a specific order, to do certain things as soon as possible. Or at least, for me, there was that weird pressure to present how I would, like super masculine as a guy, and I'm obviously a little more nonconforming.

Dani: You're definitely a little more rainbow.

Hold On To Your Child (Within)

By Uilliam Joy Bergman

My name is Uilliam (Liam) Joy and I am seventeen. To write this essay, I chose a couple of lines from famous poems, quotes, and a of couple themes from this book, to help ground my thinking about trusting kids.

> "It takes courage to grow up and become who you really are."
> —e.e. cummings

I do not like the idea that it takes courage to grow up. Firstly, there's the thing where we are always becoming, we never fully arrive. We're constantly on a path of discovery; we never arrive at this imagined ideal of "adulthood." So this line just instantly goes against that idea. Secondly, to say that first you grow up, and then you become an adult, and then you find out who you are, is undermining that kids already know who they are. Besides, it's kind of saying: now you are this person and you're stuck as that person forever... Saying that you have to be courageous, because growing up is so hard, but actually, in truth, I think the thing that shows huge strength in people and inner courage, is being able to stay a kid. And despite being older, say an adult, being able to continue to have fun is important for a thriving life. It also suggests that kids are not smart yet. They're not cool. That you got to grow up and become a better person, and then you become mature. And, you know, it takes courage to get to that point. And to me, I just say no! Because those people at the end of the day are running away from childhood. And they're thinking: I got to grow up quickly. For me, when I am older, I would rather be able to stay youthful. I always say to people that maturity is realizing that you can still be a kid ... I'm seventeen, and I'm still "immature" a lot of the time. This line is also suggesting that we just accept that we lose who we are as kids (or that it is squashed by the oppressive adult world). This notion causes the terrible situation we are in: Parents, a lot of times, are so cut off from their childhood selves that they forget what it is like to be a kid, and then some of them treat kids terribly, and then the patterns continue. I've said this my whole life: many adults cut out their childhood memories and really don't want to remember childhood. And not just because something bad happened but because they think they can't embrace that time, be childlike. And that's why some end up being terrible parents, or treat kids badly.

You have to remember what it's like to be a kid If you want to be good with kids. Of course, some might have had a terrible childhood and don't really have much of a connection to being a kid. But you can still, as an adult, explore being childish and reconnecting with the wonder of being young. So, through this process of being in the thought process of a kid, it will heal you and help connect you to kids today. Yet, most adults don't want to go near that, they don't want that anymore. I think it takes courage to stay connected to your child self, and not fall into the norms of society.

The next one is a few lines from the very popular poem, "On Children" by Kahlil Gibran.

> Your children are not your children.
> They are the sons and daughters of Life's longing for itself.
> They come through you but not from you,
> And though they are with you yet they belong not to you.
> You may give them your love but not your thoughts,
> For they have their own thoughts…
> You may strive to be like them, but seek not to make them like you.[1]

Reading these lines felt a bit like a roller coaster, because it went from good to bad to good to bad to good. Yes, the kids are not yours *per se,* you do not "own" them. And yes, don't make them like you. But also tell your kids your thoughts! Like, no, don't just let your kid run freely with their own thoughts, they're kids, they need guidance. Also, if you gave birth: they did come from you, you're their parent. I get the poetry of coming through you, etc., but let's

---

1   Kahlil Gibran, "On Children," in *The Prophet* (New York: Alfred A. Knopf, 1923), 3–8, 11. References are to line.

just not make this weird. I agree with the part "don't make your kids be just like you, they're their own people." Yes. It reminds me of how parents can also mirror their kids. It's a relational dynamic. It's generally seen that kids will mirror their parents' behaviors and ways of being in the world. And what a lot of people don't seem to realize, or accept, is that parents sometimes will mirror the stuff that kids do as well, even so-called neurotic behaviors. So, if the kid is having all these hard things going on in their lives, sometimes the parents will mirror that. Kids deserve autonomy and consent, and to be listened to, but not this strange idea of full freedom (whatever that is). Because they need the adults to provide guidance, tell them their thoughts, and give concrete care! It's like, if a baby is crying PICK THEM UP! Don't just let them cry alone. Because being alone in those moments causes trauma and they're going to develop heavy insecurities and fear. When a parent leaves a baby to cry alone they're seeding distrust in those moments.

But it's hard. You're going to make mistakes, we all do in relationships. But you have to find some kind of balance of taking care of the kids while also giving them autonomy to be themselves. The polar extremes are neglect and helicopter parenting. But there's these beautiful spaces in between where you're giving, you're guiding, you're listening. What I am referring to is kids under nine, or so. It's different for each kid. But usually when they get to nine or ten, they will need to individuate more, and be trusted more, they become even more of their "own person." But you still have to take care of them! The world is ageist and hard, so if they still want to sleep in the bed with you, let them because they're young and going through hormonal changes now and they need your support. But no matter the age, they're always learning with and from you. They learn about the world through what their parents are doing. So if you're not showing up for your kid and giving them your thought process and stuff like that, the kids are going to go through life confused and not trust anyone because their first source of trust didn't do anything for them. So, yes, your kids have their own thoughts, but they also learn from you and everyone around them. It's your responsibility as an adult to be present and generous with your thoughts—of course, we learn from each other.

> "Trust Children. Nothing could be more simple—or more difficult.
> Difficult, because to trust children we must trust ourselves—and most
> of us were taught as children that we could not be trusted."
> —John Holt, *How Children Learn*

This is good. It's so real, because yes kids are not trusted, and then they grow up feeling like they have to treat their kids that way too. I have noticed in my wider community and online that there are many teens and young adults who seem to hold grudges against kids. And it really comes from that place of hurt, that place of feeling like they weren't trusted as kids and had hard childhoods. So now when they see kids being trusted and having a good time, they feel jealous and terrible about it. And so, if we all just trusted kids from the start, we wouldn't actually even get bad parenting in the future. It's a terrible feedback loop where the parent is triggered and hurt and so replicates it. And I get that, but I also want to say, just drop your bullshit for a second! Your kids trust you, and it'll grow and you'll be happier if you trust your kids back.

I had said this line below to my mom when I was nine. With my consent she and Nick put it in their book *Joyful Militancy*, so I thought I would ponder on it now.

> "I don't need to be empowered by adults; I need them to stop having
> power over me."

I said this in response to a workshop for kids that was being offered, and it said EMPOWERING KIDS! And it just bugged me. But, at the end of the day, I think my thought process then was this feeling of the adults forcing me to have power. I thought: why can't I choose when to have power? I still agree with my response. It's good to talk about power and share it. But I think it also gets conflated with responsibility. If adults are working with kids, yes, the kids should have the same amount of power that adults have, but the adults also need to hold the most responsibility for creating a safer space and providing care. Also, there's this dynamic where activists are always trying to get more power, but we shouldn't want to replace one power with another one, or make another kind of power the supremacy. Because that's just falling back into empire. And then, by doing that, we're teaching our kids how to live out systems of hierarchy.

I do agree that kids should have more power. And it's happening more often; kids are getting more power now. There's so much stuff happening now, more freedoms, more listening, but it's still very bad out there for many kids. This idea of empowering kids can be rigid by how it's measured, for instance I often hear "Let's give kids total control!" Sure, give kids control, but maybe don't give anyone *full* control. Really don't give kids *full* control because they're still kids. They need guidance from adults, not control. The guidance needs to be respectful and consent-based. But what would full power/control even mean? Putting a kid in full control will cause most kids to panic and feel burdened. It's the opposite of thriving.

Trust Kids! was originally going to be called *Solidarity Begins at Home,* so I want to respond to that idea.

Solidarity at home is essential. There is a direct link between how much solidarity is at home and how kids engage in relationships when they go to school, or out into the world. If they're not getting any solidarity (meaning they are not being listened to, believed, trusted, cared for, etc.) in their most important relationships at home, how will they be empathetic and kind to others? At its worst, I think that when bullying is seeded, at home by a bully parent or adult, it's adults who are not in solidarity with them. Sometimes it's subtle: maybe there was no solidarity because their parents weren't ever in a good mood, and were never great to them by being open and listening. Then kids will have a hard time being in a good, generous mood either; the lack of care reverberates. It's not a binary. And, you know, bullying is terrible, but I've never once said, all that a bully deserves is to get punished or something, because it's because they're hurting—they're not getting the solidarity at home to feel safe, to feel loved. They need love.

In my home we had solidarity happening all the time. It's between us all and it's messy and there's so much compromise. To support all of us by hearing us and meeting our needs, that's work! But because I always felt that solidarity, the trust, I never went down a path of ever feeling like I had to lash out at my peers, to take out my issues on other people and be shitty to other people. Because my family didn't reflect that on me.

You know, it does take a lot of practice to do it well. And it's rewarding. I think that's what sparks in me, at least when I think of that saying "solidarity begins at home." I think of how it affects youth and their every day when they leave their house. And it really all does begin at home.

What it means to be part of a web of healing and love

To wrap this up, I want to write a bit about the importance of community, intergenerational mentorship, and relationships in general that all work to support each other to heal and thrive, and feel like we all belong, and are all loved.

I grew up in and around a large, incredible intergenerational community. These intergenerational relationships are really important to talk about and experience because so many of my peers did not have this and they feel all alone. I also think their parents feel/felt alone. So many of the young people in my life have an innate fear around most adults; they don't trust them and often can't look them in the eyes, or they feel judged—they definitely want to escape their presence as quickly as they can... I've had a lot of friends who couldn't even stand seeing a nice relationship in a show between an adult and a kid because they think something creepy/pedophilic is going to happen, because that's instantly where their mind goes, because of how shitty society has been around all of that. And, you know, I wish we could all shift this, because I think a relationship between a five-year-old and eighty-year-old is really important. I think that's a really important friendship to build, and the mentorships that grow from relationships across ages is really important. But the way society keeps showcasing the terrible stories is a problem. Like, it can only happen if the adults are in power and controlling the kid, or something like that. Or showing that kids growing up have fear around adults...

I'm glad I was surrounded by adults and a community of all ages, and all the trust that flowed was normal. I can actually hang out with adults and parents and not feel scared. And that's a good feeling. I wish other youth I knew growing up were able to have that. But often the adults around them didn't trust them. It's really important to trust the kids and help the kids, but it's also important to help the parents too, to give concrete support and help them figure out what they need as well, because everyone's human and everyone needs support!

I think trauma really cuts people off from even knowing who they are, let alone knowing what they need, or what their kids need. Without a community of support around, you feel alone, and the parents can get clouded with anger and fear and it just spirals down. My main wish is that people were able to help and be helped more easily—both the kids and the parents. I think in those situations, adults, especially those caring for children need to stop blaming their kids for their issues and look at themselves, reach out and get help, and realize that maybe they have trauma and need to heal. I do think one way to heal is to recover your child within, and think about your childhood—break the narratives! Maybe there were good times, and think about times when adults in your young life were good to you, and hold on to that, and then it will grow for your kid too.

Also, life can be hard on all of us, and there's a good chance your kids are hurting too, even in a radical, trusting, solidarity-filled home. Transphobia is real, racism is real, ableism is real, ageism is real... It affects each of us in different degrees of seriousness, but we are all affected in some way. I think mental health is super important to highlight. There have been many times where my friends tell their parents that they are depressed, but the parents are shocked and try to belittle it, or demand to know why, and most kids can't answer that. Most adults can't either! I always think back to when I first told my mom that I was depressed, and at that time I was just coming out as trans masc and queer, and dealing with some hard interpersonal friendships, and she just immediately believed me and started to support me. They even said, "I would be surprised if you weren't a bit depressed, shit's hard!" Of course we weren't talking about clinical depression, that's serious, but also it just needs to be believed and helped, too. Even though my mental health stuff has been difficult, I was able to be cared for in deep ways because of the large community circling my family. I had a good foundation of trust and solidarity at home, and not just with my parents but with my brother too, who is ten years older than me. I also had other adults I could turn to, and community in general. But I think the trust with my brother was the best thing for helping me feel safe and connected. I don't feel like he's just some random older brother who I barely know, we are friends and family. Kin.

In all situations, it's not up to the kid to figure this stuff out, parents need to step up and start by listening and trusting. They also need to deal with their issues, too. But what we all need is a big beautiful intergenerational community around us to ensure we all are heard, trusted, and thriving.

Intuiting Autonomy: An interview with Yasamin Holland and Tim Holland

By carla joy bergman and chris time steele

carla: Tell us who you all are.

Tim: We met on Telegraph Ave in Berkeley in 2001, and have pretty much been together since then, living in many places: Oakland, Barcelona, Denver, Northern Arizona, and now Maine. Yasamin is an educator and artist, I am is a hip-hop artist and podcaster. We had our first kid, Winston, in Denver, but wanted to live a more nature-based holistic life, so we decided to move back east in the summer of 2018. We had our second kid, Daisy, in 2019 and we all live together on a little farm in Brunswick, Maine, a coastal college town just north of Portland.

carla: How does the relationships with your kids connect to your radical ideals, or your anti-authoritarian politics? And, how do you talk about power?

Tim: For me, having kids has rounded out some of the edges of my politics and shown a lot of holes in how I've thought about struggle or revolution or even life… Raising a family is one of the greatest and most important things we can do, because our own actions are so small against what we are facing, and everything we seek to dismantle has and will require generations. That doesn't mean our kids are going to pick up the fight from where we leave off, but they are the inheritors of the legacy of our combined struggle, and if we raise them right they'll carry those experiences into the future, in their own way, to meet the times they have been born into. Our kids are super young, so we don't get too heavy handed or theoretical with them when we talk to them about stuff. An important thing for me is that we're trying to teach them by our examples, not by telling them how things are and what to believe. The kids will come to their own conclusions about the world; it's our job to be their guides and support them in the process. Lately they ask "why?" to everything I say, and out of respect for them I always tell them. So not taking authority for granted feels like a huge part of that, but also they see us living a life rooted in the land with a sense of freedom and adventure, and we've slowed down with our work so that we could be there for our kids. Hopefully that bares fruit for them and for our relationships together!

carla: You two collaborated on other things together, like making music, can you talk about that a bit, and how it might have informed your collaboration as parents?

Tim: We haven't really made any music together since having kids. It was really just a project for fun, and we'll return to it when we have more free time! Although we've collaborated on a number of things throughout our lives, nothing prepared us to be parents(!).

carla: How do you cultivate connections with your kids?

Tim: I try to encourage them to do everything we can together that is part of our homesteading life—making fires in the morning, harvesting food, planting things, moving things around the yard, playing in the greenhouse—they lose interest at a certain point but they keep playing. When I'm making music they'll often bust in on me, sometimes Winston will want to listen on the headphones when I'm recording (so I had to start saying "fuck" less). We try to go on little adventures often, even if it's just seasonal stuff like pumpkin patches, apple picking, etc. We go to the beach a lot. We listen to what the kids are interested in and take them to do things they enjoy. Winston loves trains so we take him to ride the Narrow Gauge train a lot, Daisy loves the children's museum so now that the pandemic has settled down a bit, we try to go there more. We cook together sometimes. Their attention wanes during a lot of these activities, so we just let 'em do what they want. We build lots of Legos together. We read to them. Basically we try to always be "present" with our kids; one of us is always with them. We listen to them and engage them with respect, and try to figure out what truly moves them and then do more of that.

carla: What do you learn most from your kids?

Tim: The simple joys of life. The need to be in the moment, because they grow up so fast and if you aren't paying attention you'll miss something important. I've learned more about trucks and shit like that than I've ever wanted to know! One of my favorite anecdotes was that, on her own, Daisy figured out (while she was teething) that she could chew wintergreen leaves to sooth her gums. She saw her brother chewing wintergreen leaves and did the same. One day I was like "wtf is she eating?" so I opened her mouth and she had chewed the leaves down to a sort of gum and was using it medicinally… She figured that out on her own! Sometimes us adults just need to get out of the way and let the kids have their natural connection to things that modernity tries to strip from all of us!

carla: What does the idea of kids' inner and outer lives mean to you?

Yasamin: My hope is that my children learn to be their own best friends, and a rich inner life is part of that, a feeling of being at home in many different situations. Spending time in nature, singing and creating and dancing, adventuring, reading books and connecting to literature, having fun together and alone, laughing at ourselves and each other, these are all experiences that build an inner life. Curiosity, wonder, and observation are mainstays of our daily experience that foster the idea that life is an adventure and there are always connections to make within ourselves and between ourselves, and the world around us. As artists and partners in parenting, Tim and I are very enthusiastic and supportive of whatever our children are into. You like Brio trains? Great! You like vegan yogurt? Great! I am passionate about encouraging my children to pursue their interests, what feeds their inner lives.

I'm also really into teaching about intuition. I am a very intuitive person and think humans have devolved to ignore our intuition. I talk to my children about their inner voice and wisdom, and trusting in the sensations and clues from their bodies. Intuition can be this great, empowering tool, connected—I believe—to our inner lives.

"Outer lives" makes me think of connection and community and the various ways kids interact with the world around us.

carla: Is there a difference with how you are with young folks as a teacher/ educator vs. a parent? If so, in which ways? If not, please explain why.

Yasamin: I had a mentor whose philosophy was that adults have to foster in ourselves the same qualities we hope to teach in young people. I believe that.

It's hard sometimes! Teaching and parenting are alike in that they hold up a mirror to the self. Both are an opportunity to grow and change and to continue to be more open and less controlled by ego. In both experiences, I reflect a lot on what I think I did well: When did I connect well? What was successful? And where can I do better and be more intentional in my approach? Teaching art and parenting two young children are a double whammy jackpot for someone like me who loves psychology and who is invested in personal growth and development, and the positive ripple effects that result.

It is a privilege to teach young people. I have a blast. I like to enjoy my days, and while that isn't realistic every day, my goal is to be deeply present in my interactions. Presence means that I get a lot out of my interactions; I allow myself to learn as much as I teach. I care about active listening and reflecting back the positive qualities I experience in my students, and the same is true for my children. I prioritize joy and belonging in teaching and parenting.

carla: How do you nurture very young kids to have a voice, and to truly feel heard and believed?

Yasamin: I experience my children as individuals, not as an extension of myself. This is helpful! We include our children in the decisions that shape their days, whether about what to eat, what to do, where to go. We solicit their thoughts, feelings, opinions, and questions throughout the day. We are open to their ideas and create a lot of space for their life experience, including all the emotions and the various expressions of emotions that come up throughout the day. As someone who grew up feeling like I had to earn love and respect, my hope is that my words and actions communicate that I respect and love my children unconditionally. Part of that means allowing them to show up however they want and need to show up, and being self-aware enough to know that if I feel irritated it has less to do with their behavior, and instead creates an opportunity for me to self-reflect and shift away from reactivity. Our children participate in daily activities, often helping with cooking and gardening and household chores, including "washing" dishes. You can feel that they feel they are a part of something, that their role in this thing we are doing over here, this life we are living… they help make it work.

Also, language has power. I'm spouting affirmations left and right and phrases like I believe you, you know yourself so well, your voice matters, your opinion matters, your feelings matter, you are a wonderful teacher… it comes from a place of deep respect.

carla: What does empathy mean to you, particularly in how you respond to your kids' feelings and perspectives?

Yasamin: I don't try to change their feelings or manage their feelings, or how they manifest in real time. They don't need to follow an arbitrary rule book of what is acceptable to express and feel, or when and where it is appropriate to feel and express. Recently, Winston and I were in the checkout line at Whole Foods and he was exhausted and crying and flopping and loud, and half the groceries were unloaded from the cart, and leaving didn't feel like an option. I felt stressed and rushed and confused about what to do, but I took some deep breaths, smiled and shrugged at the cashier, and kept saying to Winston that he helped with the groceries, and we were almost done, and somehow we made it out of the store, and Winston was perfectly fine once he got to the car. When they are upset, I ask myself questions like, "Are they hungry?" "Are they tired?" And I will ask them, "What do you need right now?" I validate their feelings and offer support, which may look like them screaming and crying on the couch alone for five minutes while I say calmly from the doorway, "I am here for you if you need me." It's amazing how transformative a good cry can be! Sometimes that's all they need.

I make space for their dissent. I respect their dissent and encourage them to listen to their inner voice at home and in the world, especially my son who is in school. If I've said no to something and they communicate a solid case for an alternative, I often change my mind. I hold fast to boundaries of safety and personal comfort, and some others relating to family culture—for example, you only get one snack after dinner—but I know as an educator and parent that boundaries help children feel safe. We make space for the dissent that comes up sometimes when boundaries are set, but that doesn't change the boundary.

So much of my own upbringing was focused on socialization and appearances. I am continually trying to unlearn and undo that mode of thinking, and parenting provides the perfect opportunity to practice. If I find myself feeling embarrassed or upset by something they do, I'm thinking of public parenting here, I think of it as an opportunity to actively change course in my thought process, and instead focus on how I can creatively connect with my child.

Final note: I credit the *Upbringing* podcast and the *Unruffled* podcast as touchstones for topics such as navigating big emotions in young people. I've read a lot of books and enjoy thinking and reading about parenting philosophy. It's fun for me. It has helped me tremendously.

carla: How has making art, specifically your music, connected to your relationship with your kiddos? What does love mean to you?

Tim: Before Winston could even walk, I had a circuit bent keyboard he'd play with on the floor of my studio. Both kids have grown up barging in on me in the studio, making beats, dancing to music while I'm writing, "jamming," just enjoying pressing the buttons and twisting the knobs. It's definitely rubbed off because Winston is just constantly singing and freestyling. We've got lots of musical instruments around the house, music is a huge part of our life and family ritual. They have their own favorite songs and that's what we listen to in the car, on repeat. Some of the sweetest moments are when Winston wants to put headphones on and "work with me" in the studio while I'm recording.

To me, "love" is the feeling of really caring about someone and having a deep connection to them. It's about treating that person with care and respect, being there for them, and growing together.

chris: You've often spoke about the value of play, with being an artist and making music, such as messing with a new plug in, playing with a keyboard for hours, and that experimentation formulating into a song. How has having kids and being a parent reopened some of those doors that may have been closed or how has it influenced your art?

Tim: I've definitely learned tons of new functions with various keyboard apps from the way Winston goes in and presses every button and opens up functions on my gear that I didn't know that the equipment had! It reminds me very much of my old friend Telephone Jim Jesus who would approach music making with a childlike curiosity and made crazy experimental music that way. But honestly, I'd say I have less time to just doodle and experiment now that I'm full-on parenting so much of the time. Much less time to experiment and play by myself in the studio. When every minute is a precious resource, it's hard to find the time to just fuck around with one keyboard setting for eight hours and stare out the window.

chris: How has your perspective changed about ongoing climate catastrophe now that you are parents?

Tim: My perspective on climate change hasn't changed, but I'm glad we moved to a less brittle place that feels a bit temporarily removed from some of the worst aspects of desertification that are sweeping the west. But we all know that no one and nowhere is safe from what is coming. That said; our kids are being raised with a connection to the land in ways that we weren't, with a sensibility of solidarity and knowledge and it's going to be up to us to figure out how we navigate the future. Hopefully our kids will bring that with them. And, if nothing else, the things they learn, the experiences they are having now, which are rooted to a sense of sustainability and deep connection to nature, will give them the tools, experience, and knowledge to navigate what is to come.

chris: Since Occupy in Denver, how have your thoughts on anarchy and autonomy expressed themselves in your life, and perhaps speak to how they effected your parenting?

Tim: Reading the book *To Our Friends* by the Invisible Committee really opened my mind to what Occupy's true flaws were and what was great about it. What was great was the connection we all had to each other, and our shared experience of rage, rebellion, and solidarity. What was wrong about it was the overall bureaucratic nature of how occupy functioned. We don't need bodies of democratic voices telling people what to do, or what they stand for. They show what they stand for in their actions, and everyone can't agree on everything all the time. I guess the same is true of kids. Through my struggles in the city of Denver, I came to the conclusion that cities were probably not fertile ground for building the sort of autonomy I imagined, especially with kids. That's why we're out here, doing what is possible to reproduce daily life on our own terms, in a joyful way that is holistic and lends itself to kids getting to experience nature in a small-town setting.

Anarchy Begins At Home

By Idzie Desmarais

> "We are all communists with our closest friends, and feudal lords
> when dealing with small children."
> —David Graeber, *Debt*

> "We can't change what we won't examine; we can't break free if we still taint our freedom
> waters with coercive relationships among the people we live with and influence most."
> —Akilah S. Richards, *Raising Free People*

Children often seem like the exception. They're one of the groups most often excluded, overlooked, and shut away from even an attempt at liberation. Once you start to pay attention to the way children are talked about and treated—or relearn to see the injustices most of us were acutely aware of as children—the constant disparagement, othering, and violence is impossible to ignore. Children are oppressed. And so the next steps must be to ask how we can fight that oppression, and to reimagine (and rediscover) the ways adults and children can relate to each other and live together in more respectful, trustful ways.

◆

I recently made the mistake of commenting in passing to my mother that our upbringing—my sister and I—was accidentally anti-authoritarian. "It wasn't an accident" was her firm response.

When I reached my teens, the gulf that existed between the way I was treated by my parents, and the way other teens I knew were, became impossible to ignore. It was far from the first time I'd considered how differently my own growing-up was progressing. After I left kindergarten to pursue a life of flexible, self-directed learning outside of school (a practice often referred to as unschooling), there were many ways my life diverged from the norm, but it was in my teens that the difference I saw in parenting—in trust—became particularly stark.

It was unquestionably my mother who shaped the environment I experienced as a child, who set the norms of respect and cooperation, who was unfailingly supportive of any interests I had, and always ready to help dig up helpful people and resources. Yet even my father, more conventional by far, became so accustomed over the years to a certain way of relating to us children that, by the time we hit our teens, ideas of surveillance and control seemed to be the furthest thing from his mind.

A partial list of things I did not experience in my teens:

- Mandated schoolwork or homework
- A curfew
- Screen limits
- Grounding
- Violations of privacy such as the reading of a diary or online messages with friends
- Rules or punishments of any sort, really

So it was that I eased into my teen years (as did my sister a couple of years later) without the parental panic, the cracking down, and the obsessing about "bad influences" I observed among other parents in the suburbs where we lived. Instead, we could generally do whatever we wanted, within the bounds of available resources and transit, our own personalities, and our own morality.

And rather than the chaos some might imagine would result, we were fine. I think it's important to remember that people's behavior always exists within their own social context. The ways that teenagers *are*—the supposedly immutable patterns of behavior culturally ascribed to teens—exist within a society in which they are oppressed, stripped of power, surveilled (by parents or other guardians, schools, and by police), criminalized, and controlled. I would suggest that basing our understanding of teenage behavior on a population existing under oppression, shut away from the rest of society in schools, with very little power or freedom, does not represent an accurate picture of what teens are innately like. I would also suggest that much of what is cast as "bad" behavior is not inherently bad; it's simply inconvenient or dangerous to power.

If environment shapes behavior, as it clearly does, then there needs to be the recognition of how very different it is to be a teenager who is trusted by adults in their lives, and how much that influences the choices they make, the relationships they have with others, the way they solve problems, and recover from mistakes. My whole experience of "no rules" combined with unschooling, was accompanied by the constant discomfort of witnessing the ways other teens were treated, how little autonomy they possessed, and how much their well-being was impacted by that fact. It was clear to me early on that there was a direct relationship between the level of authoritarianism teens experienced and the choices they made (or were forced, through circumstance, to make). Some children learned they needed to lie and hide their (often self-destructive) behavior from adults for fear of anger, punishment, and violence. Other children, those who had older people they could rely on, who would help solve problems instead of punishing them for being human and making mistakes, were inclined to be far more open and truthful. Knowing that the adults in their lives were on their side made a big difference.

An incomplete list of things I did experience as a teenager:

- Lots of free time
- Assistance with transportation and logistical organization
- Parents who would always come get me if something went wrong, or if I was uncomfortable in a situation, or if I needed help, no questions asked ahead of time and no artificially generated "consequences" doled out afterwards
- Lots of access to resources, through the Internet, library, organized activities, optional classes, and other people
- A listening ear for whatever was troubling me, a service that was extended to friends of mine as well
- Trust

In the years I have spent writing about more respectful and liberatory ways of relating to children, I have often encountered those who liken not seeking to control kids with neglect, as if adults recognizing that children are people must necessitate a lack of involvement. I imagine this is because most adults are accustomed to relating to young people entirely through a lens of control and management, and when they envision taking that away, they think there would be nothing left. Yet the recognition that children deserve trust and respect does not mean adults abdicate all responsibility toward them: instead, it means they recognize that their responsibility, with the incredible position of power they hold, is to nourish, care for, support, facilitate, and trust the young people in their lives. Easier said than done, but it is something that should be the goal of all people, of all ages, when existing in caring relationships with each other.

◆

Unconventional as their choices were, my parents were not exactly anarchic themselves (though the aforementioned anti-authoritarianism was a vital part of my mother's philosophy), but my own radical politics grew naturally out of the ideas that shaped my childhood. The dismissal, neglect, and abuse I witnessed as a teenager left a lasting anger and bitterness, as I saw kids treated in whatever ways the adults—parents, teachers, and occasionally social workers—saw fit, with little to no recourse provided to them. And I knew to my very bones that the schooling and parenting most children were subjected to, the things that just *must* be done in a certain way to produce the "right" kind of adults according to popular wisdom, were simply unnecessary; unneeded at best, damaging at worst, and far from the only way to exist in the world.

By the time I was a teenager, I'd spent years making a lot of my own choices, without every moment being scheduled and dictated by adults, and I feel that in some ways this time functioned as an inoculation against the belief that others had the right to hold authority over me. Within more hierarchical activities or situations, I was generally a rule-follower (a quiet, shy child who didn't really wish to be singled out), but it was conditional. It didn't follow me out of those specific activities, didn't impact how I saw adults in general, and it didn't lead me to think adults were entitled to throw their weight around just by virtue of their age. In an environment where adults ruled, if the downsides outweighed the benefits, I could quit, and leave, and that was it.

◆

Children are usually prevented from choosing how to spend their own time— nominally for their own good, more accurately for the good of capitalism and the state—because they are not trusted to be adequately productive, to shape themselves into the workers they are required to be, so that job must naturally fall instead to the adults (most often, though not limited to, parents and teachers). Children, left to their own devices, will be "lazy" and "unproductive," will "waste" their time (and by extension, their lives) in sloth and idleness. I think it is crucial for all adults who claim to resist capitalism and wage labor to fight for children's right to their own time, their rest and play and daydreaming and laying about. That a child's "laziness" must be seen as an innately human expression of autonomy and pleasure in life, a resistance to the demands placed on them to labor for others, first in the form of schoolwork and later in the form of wage labor.

Unschooling was such an integral part of my life, and enabled me to spend endless time playing, reading, writing, in group activities and in solitude, in nature and curled up in my room focused intently on a craft project, in the library and at friend's houses, on the computer and on hikes. My education meant essentially doing whatever I wished to, instead of spending years sitting at desks completing tasks chosen by authority figures, and yet what I experienced was unquestionably "education"—life learning—without any of the coercion thought to be needed to make children learn.

Once you realize that one huge area of common wisdom is false, it becomes much easier to question all of them. If children will flourish without the imposition of violent authority, why not adults? If punishment is unnecessary and damaging to children, why then is it appropriate for people of any age? Step by step, the ways that our society functions appeared more damaging, more grotesque, more unnecessary and frightening. To grow up as I did forever shaped the way I learned to see the world.

◆

Because my own entry to anarchism—to anti-authoritarian, liberatory politics—was a path that started within ideas of child-autonomy, I think I expected to see that reflected more in anarchist theory than I did then and have since. It isn't absent of course, as there exist strong critiques of schooling, and sometimes of parental authority as well. Yet often I find myself puzzled by those who claim anti-authoritarianism more broadly, and yet treat children as the exception. So often the same dynamics of adult-child relationships found in the broader culture are recreated even by radicals who treat children with disdain, or who see themselves as still holding rightful authority over them. I often find myself remembering a quote from Emma Goldman, where she observes

> Radical parents, though emancipated from the belief of ownership in the human soul, still cling tenaciously to the notion that they own the child, and that they have the right to exercise their authority over it. So they set out to mold and form the child according to their own conception of what is right and wrong, forcing their ideas upon it with the same vehemence that the average Catholic parent uses. And, with the latter, they hold out the necessity before the young "to do as I tell you and not as I do."[1]

1   Emma Goldman, "The Child and Its Enemies," *Mother Earth* 1, no. 2 (April 1906): 13.

This tendency toward child-shaping remains prevalent today, where the goal often seems to be the creation of future revolutionaries, the shaping of the product that is the child into an acceptable adult. Though the goals may be very different, the process quickly begins to look almost indistinguishable from those whose ideal result is the production of useful workers. In both cases, the child is a subject to be acted upon, not a complete human with their own desires, goals, and values, their own unique way of existing in the world.

What is needed is true child liberation, true autonomy, true trust and respect, because children deserve these things by right of being people. There doesn't have to be—there shouldn't be—any justification needed, any future use to be extracted from them, for children to be deserving of liberation.

Though there should be no plan to mold children for a desired future, there should be the recognition that to live with children as equals is itself a way of shaping the world, bringing into being through action the liberatory future that is sought. Interpersonal relationships are the bedrock of all other social relations, all other forms of organizing, all other structures. "The forcible subjugation of children by adults forms the psychological underpinning of every other model of political and economic subjugation. This is not a metaphor; it's a structuring principle of political reality,"[2] writes Carol Black, summarizing the work of Toby Rollo. So to do the work of undoing that subjugation, of pushing back against it, is in many ways to fundamentally attack the underpinnings of all the interconnected oppressions on which this colonialist, capitalist society is built.

◆

My parents were not perfect, and neither was my childhood. Mistakes were made, my needs were not always understood, my home was not always a peaceful place, my parents carried their own baggage, and my own mental illness still shaped my experiences in negative ways. I think this is important to note because I am not speaking of seeking some unreachable perfection within a deeply adultist society, but of embracing meaningful changes everyone can put into effect in their dealings with children, whether as parents, guardians, family, friends, or community members. I wish for everyone who cares about liberation to see children as whole people, who, while they may have different care needs and require different types of support from adults, are no less

---

2   Carol Black, "On the Wildness of Children," 2016, http://carolblack.org/
on-the-wildness-of-children.

whole human beings for it. Along with this can come the understanding that adults too have different needs and require different types of support, and the level of independence someone is capable of, regardless of age, should not be a reason to grant or deny them respect, trust, and autonomy.

Perfection was not needed in order for the greater trust extended to me as a young person to forever influence my life in positive ways. The ripples made by that break with authoritarianism shaped my politics, my ideas about productivity and success, my relationships, my ongoing education, and every other aspect of my life.

To trust children is to anchor ourselves to a moral foundation, a place from which a freer world can grow, as long as we're willing to help it along.

Already in My Bones

By my ancestors, me, and my kin

I am the bones of my ancestors, and the blooms of my kin. I am the compost of the land, and the life that springs from it. I am the legacy of those who walked before me, and a ghost to those who walk next. My name is not the point of this story.

I come from the land and belong to it. My mother was born in Portugal amongst the land, the people, and the poverty. Her mother, my vovo, much the same. Vovo's ancestral wisdom was always her anchor to culture, belonging, and pride. She came to so-called "Canada" at the age of twenty-six with five young children and a fourth grade education. But she was brilliant, and she taught me about where I came from and the people who came before me. She taught me to cook the foods of our ancestors. She taught me how to care for others, she taught how much we can give even when we have little, and that sharing food will always bring people together.

Growing up, aunts, uncles, cousins, and chosen family would fill my grandparents' house with laughter and chaos. Our bellies would be filled with fresh bread still warm from the oven, spicy chorizo, barbecued sardines, and the garden's fresh veggies and herbs doused in olive oil. I remember my grandfather sitting in his spot at the table, his crutches always resting in the same place behind him (he'd lost a leg in an accident not long after they came to Canada). I remember running through the garden, under the fig and plum trees, with my cousins and brothers—losing track of who was chasing who. I remember my aunts and uncles drinking my grandfather's homemade wine that flowed freely. I remember tears of joy and laughter and the booming voices of Mediterranean passion. These chaotic family dinners are some of my favorite memories, and they all revolve around my grandmother and the strength and wisdoms she held and the care she took of all of us. But I know, for her, it was her kin who gave her life.

After my grandfather passed at a young age of sixty-two, vovo's health slowly started to decline. Time passed and she fell more ill and as a result we all gathered less and less.

There isn't a happy ending to that part of my story. After a long and drawn out illness, with many brain surgeries and months in hospital, eventually we said goodbye to our vovo. Most of us grown, with lives of our own started. I was in my mid-twenties by then.

Somewhere along the way, I started absorbing dominant culture narratives of how to be a successful woman and feminist in American culture. Not to mention the untangling of family shame and process of reclamation (still ongoing) around our Indigenous identity (on my father's side) and unknown (to me) ancestors. My late teens and early twenties were weighed down with heavy critique of my peers with kids, because they chose to have kids "early." At this time, and I cringe looking back on this, I believed myself to be a radical who would change the world with my bright ideas and my dreadfully overpriced art school education. Individualism and patriarchy fueled this desire and told me I could only be a success or make a change in the world around me if I eschewed any dream of being a mother.

Throughout my early twenties, I believed a handful of myths about children—or more specifically about what having children would do to me as a feminist. Mainly the myths revolved around children being a distraction from my true and full potential as a woman, and so on. This narrative obviously is harmful for women, but more importantly, it's harmful to our children. Popular culture constantly reinforces the notion that children are a heavy burden on working mothers or on society as a whole. So much so that we've normalized mothers resenting their children in our media and stories.

Coming from working-class parents (with immigrant grandparents) I wanted so desperately to believe that I could surmount capitalism, that I could be a success if I worked hard, got good grades, went to university. And of course, as a woman, my success could look exactly like that of the cis-white men that were my peers.

The patriarchy and individualism really sell us this version of feminism that says "women can build a legacy, but not if they want to be mothers too."

But a legacy doesn't matter much if children are not safe, loved, and cared for.

Unravelling the stories of patriarchy and colonialism from my identity as a woman and from my expectations of feminism is an ongoing challenge, one that I am not always handling well.

When I first started exploring my Squamish ancestry and asking questions about Indigenous culture, I didn't really have any clear expectations. I wanted to make connections, fill in some gaps about my father's family, and maybe learn some songs and stories along the way. But what this reclamation has given me is so much more. I don't know the people who could be my direct cousins. I don't know stories from my Squamish relatives. I don't know who they were, who they loved, how they lived. But I did start to learn a way of belonging to the Land, to the Water, to the people, and to my kin—blood or not. I started to learn that a lot of the "barriers" I saw to success were only barriers in a capitalist colonial system.

I remember a conversation with my vovo when I was in university. I was just learning about Indigenous knowledge and wisdoms from around the globe and the power of ancestral teachings. I was surprised to learn how little she believed in herself and her own knowledge and wisdom. She never went beyond age ten in school and so reading and writing were never a strength of hers, but she could speak two languages fluently, could cook, could tell stories, and teach love. Our current dominant culture, which prioritizes only one type of success, one type of knowing and being, made my vovo believe she did not have a lot to offer.

Mothers are often unsuccessful in this system because it does not hold up and support them and children. We have individualized the family, cut off mothers from community supports, severed the threads that allowed children to be central to a community's capacity to thrive. We have removed the magic and gifts that motherhood and childhood are, while simultaneously undermining the value of those who choose to care for community in this way. Dominant culture in the West has a narrow vision of success that is modelled after a life that demeans and undervalues the role of women and children.

I am not an expert on Indigenous motherhood, but my intuition is rooted in listening to children and teaching them that they are gifts from the creator. Indigenous parenting is not just the responsibility of a mother; it is the community and the cultural infrastructure that should support the child through practices of mentorship, through storytelling, through passing down ancestral knowledge. This helps children understand their own role in community and enables them to connect to kinship beyond their immediate family. Ultimately, this gives them a larger support network. It allows for mothers and parents to thrive and see their children thrive too.

What I've learned from my ongoing process of reclamation of indigeneity is that all life comes from the Land and the right to that life and Land belongs to the future generations. I've learned that centering children and kinship will make our communities stronger. It taught me that I did not have to be a mother—though I ended up wanting that (all choices around this are valid, not everybody needs to want that either)—but I did have to ask myself how I could show up for the kids that were already in my life. All of which I had already been taught by my vovo.

My vovo died more than a year before I got pregnant. At that point, I was rarely visiting my family. I talked on the phone every other month or two with my parents. I was learning more about who I was, and where I came from, but along the way I forgot to actually be with the people that I came from. Having my baby brought me back to my family, not because I suddenly understood the value of family, but because I *needed* them. We are not meant to parent in isolation. I did need them, but I am also so grateful to have come back to my family. Ironically, my journey of Indigenous reclamation brought me to find confidence in an unplanned pregnancy and as a single mother, but the things it taught me about motherhood and matriarchy were already in my bones. Not just from my Squamish ancestors, but from my vovo who lived for the children in her life. I may not have stories from my Squamish ancestors to pass on to my kid, but I will teach him about where we came from, so he knows how to carry it forward. My vovo never got to meet my kid, but he will know stories of her. He will learn the wisdoms and teachings that she passed on to me. Her legacy is me, her legacy is my kid.

Solidarities of Resistance

By Curiousism Cyphers

"We are nothing if we walk alone; we are everything when we walk together in step with
other dignified feet."
—Subcomandante Marcos, *Shadows of Tender Fury*

They chant we're changing the world knowing it will lull us to sleep
This is dominator language, each letter digs a grave that's deep
Let's re-member, re-center, un-dis-member, and re-cover
We are listeners, foragers, cultivating friends, we don't need to compete, we
need each other
Should it really be called a school if its drive is discipline and kills magic?
What's being taught to stand in a silent line but a hierarchy pageant?
Every day's a school play where someone falls through the trap door tragic
Love to the ones who make detention halls ghost towns amidst whispers of
core curriculum racket
It's not ditching, we're not truant, we've had it
What's the hand that writes the hall pass but a pipe maker?
What's trust, what's love, what's solidarity but a life saver
If you take a shovel to the playground you'll find smells of bitumen and
pipelines
They tear through Indigenous land, some go to prison, they sever lifelines
What's a standardized test but them trying to make a mechanism out of you?
Scratch a principal find a budget, scratch a teacher find a cop, they want you to
scratch yourself and find one too
And love to the teachers who listen to kids and ignore principals for principles
Who dream of better worlds, who don't want reform, knowing what's stained
in blood isn't rinsible
Is it any coincidence they make you run suicides to get conditioned to
compete?

You have to grind, you have to run yourself down, those sound like synonyms for defeat

Dictionaries and underfunded libraries, populated by hypocrisy and hypocrites

Obsessed with definitions but can't define itself, a sick institution calling children sick

When we say abolition, yes, we mean high schools too

We are fungi on wild edges, we are the thorns that grew

We don't want pedagogy, we want community over competition

More of Shakur's roses from concrete, we find each other within cracks in the system

Embracing slowness, giving time, learning from human and more-than-human wisdom

We give thanks to past, present, and emerging lineages

The co-learners, playground philosophers, disrupters, builders, weavers, and resisters

Alternative to schools, Free Schools and Freeskools, unschool, deschool

Learning while doing, Windsor House, Dreamseeds, Albany Free School, and Brooklyn Free School too

Not back to school camp, Flying Squad, and YouthFx, in the distance Holt tends to a garden gate while a warbler whistles

Each action a thorn in an authoritarian's side, a crow flies and drops a purple thistle

The Power Of Unschooling: Why My Daughters Don't Go To School

By Akilah S. Richards

How does a ten-year-old Atlanta-based Black girl with Jamaican parents, shoulder-length locs, and zero interest in school become deeply immersed in the studies of Finno-Ugric language groups and Eurasian migration?[1]

It started with flags. And the Internet, of course.

Sage would come across an image of a flag, then search online to find its related country. Then, she'd see the country's name written in its national language(s) to the right on its Wikipedia page.

Seeing the languages written down nudged her toward exploring the languages themselves, and that's how she discovered that she loves languages.

But why would a ten-year-old be researching flags?

For a school project, most likely. Right?

Not in this case, because Sage, along with her twelve-year old sister, are part of a family that practices self-directed education: specifically, unschooling. Unschooling, a term coined by John Holt in the 1970s, is used to describe self-directed education, or learning that does not centralize school or a particular curriculum.

As a self-directed learner (unschooler), much of Sage's (and her sister, Marley's) time is spent exploring the things they find interesting.

Those interests, like all things in the world, do not exist in vacuums. They are connected to other things, people, and places, and so their exploration of

---

1   This essay was originally posted at Ravishly.com, December 23, 2016, https://www.ravishly .com/2016/08/26/power-unschooling-why-my-daughters-dont-go-school.

a single thing will always result in exposure to other things, the same way flag research led Sage to discover her love for languages in written form.

The catalyst for this particular interest showed up as a result of cartoon-watching. Sage and Marley are anime (Japanese animation/cartoons) enthusiasts and are constantly creating characters that they write into fan fiction versions of shows (anime) and graphic novels (manga) they enjoy.

These Original Characters (OCs)[2] were for *Hetalia*, an anime that personifies countries, and is based on the mega-popular comic and manga by Hidekaz Himaruya. Sage and Marley's OCs are incredibly detailed, and their character sheets often include the languages the characters can speak and write.

As Sage continued to create OCs, she recognized that she was particularly curious about the histories of Europe and Asia, and how migration influenced language and culture, both historically and today.

Essentially, a cartoon with no overtly embedded learning objectives was the catalyst for Sage's current studies in language, history, art, art history, geography, anthropology, and reading comprehension.

Today, she can identify multiple languages by seeing them written (Russian, Italian, Faroese, etc.). She also speaks Mandarin and is currently learning Finnish, Icelandic, and Korean.

This broadening of perspective sharpens both her understanding and her sense of ethics. For example, Sage watched and continues to watch videos about African people living in Finland, and had plenty to say about how their experiences are different from and similar to Black people from other countries living in America. She is developing a particular social justice lens as a result of her observations and opinions.

That path from exploring a single thing to diving deeper into multiple things—and discovering areas of ongoing interest—is quite normal for unschoolers. The idea is that children are given space to explore anything around them without adults guiding that exploration or requiring them to continue exploring any particular thing.

In that way, unschooling is both learning-centered and learner-centered.

What do I mean by "learning-centered" and "learner-centered"?

Unschooling is learning-centered in that it focuses on how each child learns, instead of what to teach children, or what adults believe children should be learning.

It looks at a child's approach to the world through their interactions with people, and also through their interactions with things (toys, animals,

---

2   "Original Character," Fanlore.org, https://fanlore.org/wiki/Original_Character.

television, radio, the computer, a phone, etc.). We do not test our children to gauge whether they are learning either.

We just live together and communicate, and we partner with our daughters when they need our help. Through that, we get to see the ways they are learning and growing and understanding themselves, along with the vast array of information and options for continuing their education.

This practice is learner-centered because these observations help parents know what resources they can offer their child to enable them to pursue their interests and follow their curiosity. You might be wondering where all this talking and learning is happening.

Is it during our kids' rare break from all-day gaming?

While making granola?

During lunch on our mountainside farm?

While trying to ensure our children don't grow up to become uneducated, ill-adjusted, long-term starving artists?

Ah yes, the misconceptions about unschoolers are easy to find, especially online. Media tends to portray unschoolers in a narrow and unfavorable light.

Let's address some of the more common myths:

Myth #1: Only qualified teachers can help children learn

Unschoolers own their learning, and unlike homeschooling, there is no particular curriculum or set timeframes for learning. It can happen alone, or in collaboration with other people of mixed ages in different settings (like parks).

It can happen in ad hoc learning communities (like get-togethers in homes or group chats on Skype), or pre-defined learning spaces (like libraries or virtual spaces).[3]

Similar to schools and homeschooling environments, unschooling does not look the exact same way in every setting. It's an approach to living and learning that is custom-fitted based on each family's preferences and environment.

Some unschoolers use textbooks, and others do not. Some unschoolers, like Lainie and Miro, use travel to foster learning and build community.

Other unschooling families, like Tamika Middleton's and Zakiyya Ismail's, have firm roots in one particular city, and use unschooling as a vehicle for

---

3   See for example, Crash Course, YouTube video, https://www.youtube.com/user/crashcourse.

social justice activism at home and in their local communities. This happens as their days involve practicing anti-oppressive, non-coercive approaches to parenting and in non-parent/child relationships, which is a primary tenet of self-directed education in general.

In this way, our practice explores how some beliefs and actions can negatively impact other people, and explores ways we and other people might navigate those spaces.

Myth #2: Children cannot be socialized without school

When adults address "the socialization issue," in the context of unschooling and homeschooling, what I think they really mean to ask is: How will your children know how to deal with real-world shit?

Real-world shit is unavoidable, I promise. From fights with neighborhood children, to being called names, to working in group settings, to managing personality differences... Our girls have experienced all of that. It seems to be a byproduct of living in a city populated by more than one family, and as luck would have it, we're covered.

In case you're craving more detail, Idzie Desmarais broke it down quite well in "The Ultimate Unschooling Socialization Post."[4]

Myth #3: Unschoolers can't go to college

First, not all unschoolers desire to go to college. In our home, for example, we do not encourage our daughters to get college-ready. Higher education is one of many routes to skill acquisition and peer networking, but is marketed as the best bet for any *good* parent. People who went to college (like my husband and I) will spend decades indebted to student loan funders to pay for degrees we may never use.

Our daughters know that they own themselves, and if they choose college, they know they'll have our support.

Secondly, because unschooled children aren't mired in classwork and homework for the majority of their days, they have time to act on their interests, and start

---

4   Idzie Desmarais, "The Ultimate Unschooling Socialization Post," *I'm Unschooled. Yes, I Can Write,* July 25, 2014, http://yes-i-can-write.blogspot.com/2014/07/the-ultimate-unschooling-socialization.html.

actively practicing the skills they will need in their career(s) of interest. In essence, they use real-world experiences to obtain the skills many people pay for in college.

Sure, there are career paths that call for college, and if unschooled children choose one, they simply study and test into a school, much like traditionally-schooled children.

For an interesting article on unschoolers and college, and a study by developmental psychologist and longtime self-directed education activist, Peter Gray, see Luba Vangelova's "How Do Unschoolers Turn Out?"[5]

Myth #4: Unschoolers have no friends

And by "friends," it seems many parents mean "the children their children have to see every day because they're in the same class."

Would that mean, then, that all my co-workers at my corporate gigs are now officially my friends?

Obviously not, because proximity isn't the same thing as connection.

Our daughters have what they call "Internet homies" with whom they play, learn, collaborate, and engage. Sometimes, those homies become friends; mostly, they don't. They've also formed in-person bonds with people (of all ages) who they've met along our travels throughout the Southern US and much of the island of Jamaica.

They stay in touch through Skype, FaceTime, and WhatsApp when we're not in their cities, and they meet in-person when we are.

At the end of the day, unschooling is about confidence, compassion, and agency.

Unschooling, much like democratic schools or learning co-ops, is about building mutually respectful relationships and fostering learning among people and environments—regardless of age, race, class, gender identity, sexuality, or the myriad other ways people live and identify.

For my family, this means our primary job is to answer our daughters' questions (and ask them plenty, too). Along with that, we encourage creative approaches to problem solving, and we challenge them to explore fears and—sometimes—to push past them.

We involve them in many daily aspects of adult life so they can observe, question, learn from, and challenge what they see and hear.

We do not believe that we can come from an entirely different era—particularly in terms of how information is received today—and still prepare them

---

5   See https://www.kqed.org/mindshift/37091/how-do-unschoolers-turn-out.

for the future. Preparation for the future is their job, and we help them to see options for doing that while learning how to use their interests to develop skills, to help people, to develop compassion, and to excel in whatever ways they want to live, learn, and earn.

Take Back Your Kids

By Meghan Carrico

This is an essay responding to the question: what would I say to parents and educators who are stepping into trusting their kids?

It isn't easy to listen to your child over the voices of authority. Whether the authorities are the school system, your parents, the government, or the establishment, we are told that without a standardized education children will fall economically and socially behind. If we send our children to school at least they will have—or not have—what everyone else does.

Yet, the cracks in the system are large now. Finding that niche to get a toe hold and starting your own version of listening to your kids has never been more possible.

It is often terrifying to make decisions based on your own gut feelings or your reaction to what you think is wrong with a system—especially when you have no idea of what you will do instead. That is where my story began.

My mother, Helen Hughes, was a public school teacher in 1963, the year I was born. In her first year of teaching, at the age of nineteen, she taught a class of forty-five students. She had one year of "Normal School" teacher training before becoming a teacher, and had received a home-ec scholarship for making creamy eggs, which helped to pay for her schooling. When I was born five years later, she had figured out how to keep her cloak room tidy (the sure way to tell if you were a good teacher), and had her students so well trained that she could leave them alone in the hallway staring straight ahead in a line, and no one dared to turn their head to see if she was still there. This was all that was expected, and she was considered good at her job.

After my younger brother was born, she quit teaching and eventually became a preschool teacher. Her experience at the preschool changed her view of teaching forever. She experienced children eager to learn, children whose curiosity fueled their exploration of ideas and creativity. She saw their thinking and learning flourish in an environment where they could learn through play.

At the end of my brother's time at her preschool, my mother approached a group of parents from the school to see if they would consider joining with her to open a small school for their children. This was when I was in grade two. All year I had been complaining of stomach aches and illness, starting on Sunday evening and continuing all week until Friday after school. My best friend at that time lived on my block and her mother let us come home for lunch occasionally. We would start art projects over lunch and plead to be able to stay home for the afternoon and finish them. I can't remember if we were ever allowed to do this, but we must have been at least once, because we were ever hopeful that we could again.

I was bored by school, although I couldn't have articulated it that way at the time. I liked to talk and move around the classroom. This was never allowed, except at the one time a week where we had a project of our "choice" to work on. I remember this well because mine was a crochet project out of string that didn't inspire me at all and I spent the whole time moving around and helping other students with their projects and chatting. The teacher eventually called me out on my lack of progress, and I don't have any further memories of project time after that.

It was 1971, and girls had just been allowed to wear pants to school for the first time, as long as they were part of a matching outfit. Hitting children was just going out of fashion in schools at this time and I only feared my teacher for her ability to chastise me in front of the class for daydreaming, or to give me more hard and boring worksheets to complete.

That summer, my mother, some parents from her preschool, and a few neighbors decided to open a school in our house for the fall of 1971. I don't remember any of the lead up, only that I didn't have to return to school that year, and instead I had fifteen friends show up at my house every day to play. It was heaven.

I think everyone knew what they didn't want for their children but no one really knew exactly what they *did* want. They didn't want an authoritarian, institutional, educational experience for their kids. Helen had read A. S. Neill's *Summerhill* and later John Holt's *How Children Fail*, but they didn't know a model to follow, except they wanted to follow the idea that children should have a say in their schooling.

What I remember were the art activities, beading and candlemaking (it was the 1970s), and lots of playing outside in the backyard and neighborhood. The school was run on consensus and there was a school meeting to handle any problems. These meetings were called "problem solving sessions," and you could call another student to a problem solving session, or have a whole-school problem solving session. Both required everyone named to show up and come up with solutions to your problem until we could find one that everyone agreed to. Consensus.

I learned to be able to sit through these meetings the longest, which meant I often got my way, since most of the other students became bored and just wanted to get back to playing. It worked well enough with my mom as the teacher, as she had to agree as well. She genuinely worked with us to find often-creative and unexpected solutions. She also agreed to our various punitive solutions when they didn't involve anything too drastic. These often looked like a version of "time out" or being made to sit in the corner. We called them stool penalties, where if you left a mess or some other infraction, you had to sit on a stool for fifteen minutes and occasionally up to an hour. These consequences, as they were called, were devised by us, the students. The consequences didn't seem to change our behavior much but the threat of another problem solving session did! It certainly gave me a lasting experience of the futility of punishment as a means to deterrence.

As for learning and the curriculum: we played all day. The parents conferred and talked about educational theories, made lunch every day, and occasionally set up field trips. At least this is what I remember. At one point it was decided that Helen (my mom) would give each child a twenty-minute tutorial each day to teach some basics, math and reading. This meant that all day long one of us would be called to work with Helen, leaving the rest of us to play. It was like pulling teeth because none of us ever wanted to leave the rest of the group (who were all busy playing) to go off and get a tutorial on something we weren't really interested in.

Finally, after the first year, half the parents went down the block to start a more structured school in one of their houses, and another group of parents went to Mexico to live in a cave and run a school were the students were given pocket money each day to go to town and buy their own food and take care of themselves, and my mom was left with my brother and me and one other family who had moved from California to put their children in our tiny school.

My mom says she would have given up then if she didn't feel responsible to that family. So somehow she opened that fall with a few more children and carried on. The school had been temporarily named Windsor House after the street our house was on. We had no idea at the time that the name would stick, and that, by accidentally sounding like a toney private school, we would fly under the radar and miss all of the stigma associated with many of the free schools of time, often named "Ideal School" or "The Free School," etc.

Forty-eight years later, when the school finally closed, the name had remained the same, although the philosophy meandered around a bit, but it basically stuck to its Free School roots.[1]

The key experience for me as a child was that I was celebrated. My desire to create, talk, move my body, help others learn, and participate in the governance of my community, was supported by the adults around me, and the structure of our little school in our house. Homeschooling was not the movement it is now. Perhaps if it had been, my mother would never have been approached to start a school. I appreciate that I was able to grow up in a community of children and adults who shared the creation of a school. I thrived in a small-scale, play-based, learning environment.

Windsor House taught me that you do not have to force children to learn. There are many ways to engage with learning as a community of students, parents, and teachers. Often when students choose to engage with more formal learning it is a matter of acquiring the conventions of literacy and numeracy. Our experience at Windsor House has shown me that students do learn literacy and numeracy skills over time, given a supportive and enriching environment, with teachers who can teach without judgement or comparative assessment.

Students came to learning formal academics after many years of learning through play. They asked teachers and their parents for tutoring and lessons. It was remarkable how, decade after decade, students would ask for classes to "catch them up" with their peers in conventional school, right about the same age—somewhere between ten and thirteen. It would take about a year, three mornings a week, to teach math and writing skills, and a general overview of social studies and science concepts, that brought these students up to grade level.

---

1   Windsor House ran as a private school in our house for four years. In 1975, the parents and Helen took a proposal to our local school board to have Windsor House adopted by the school district as a one room program. That year it became publicly funded and free for all of the families. The school grew to sixty students over the next few years. Around 1990, the parents of the school wanted it to extend into the high school years. Again, they started the high school as a private school and after two years applied to the school district to have it publicly funded as an extension of Windsor House. After a bit of a political campaign to get the school trustees to vote in favor of this, we were eventually successful. The school gradually grew to two hundred students over the next decade and continued with bumps and turns along the way. It was finally closed in 2019 due to financial reasons beyond our school districts' control.

Alumni students reference a moment in their early teens where a switch goes on in their head and suddenly they realize that they want some skills to be independent, and to be able to engage with mainstream schooling should they choose. This led many students to choose to attend more mainstream schooling in their middle school years, and a few chose to stay at Windsor House. Either way, students came to their own understanding of what it means to be educated.

What I would like to hold out to parents and educators who are embarking on trusting the youth in their lives, is that you don't have to know exactly how to do this in order to start. Sometimes it is choosing to listen, choosing to believe your child, to believe that it isn't them who are sick, but instead maybe it's the institutions that we are handing them over to that are sick.

When my mother took me out of school, I stopped feeling sick all week. She did not pathologize me, instead she asked herself if there was something better she could offer. She listened to her friends who were seeing the curiosity and genuine interest in learning of their children, and wanting to keep that alive. It was a time of experimentation, and voices were coming out and offering alternate possibilities.

Fifty years later, we have Covid-19, and schools that are taxed to a breaking point. Now warehousing children in rooms that can't provide two meters of space around their bodies is suddenly a safety concern. Now the curriculum is being taught remotely, and less of it, in order to deal with the crisis. Now teachers are being told that they are essential service workers, not because they are needed to teach children, but because we can't function as a society without the childcare public education provides. This is not in the best interest of children. They deserve better. What can we learn from this?

Backing parents who decide to trust their kids

As people who listen to children, who trust their kids, we do not have to raise our children in isolation. It is not the only option. Find your people, listen to other voices. It is possible to start a school in your home with five other families. You don't need to be a teacher to support your child's learning. The myth of the "core curriculum" and the need for it to be taught at a certain rate and in comparison to other children of the same age, is part of the legacy of industrial schooling. There are tools, skills, and services that are available to support families and educators to find ways to support learning at home, in learning centers, across countries, virtually, in-person, and in community.

The homeschooling movement has given individual families who could afford to have their children stay home, a way to say "no" to institutionalizing their children. The next movement needs to be supporting families and educators who don't want to institutionalize their children, but who can't afford to homeschool, who need childcare, and who want a community for their children to learn in.

It can be done. Consider the ingenuity and resourcefulness of my mother. She can tell you about teaching night school to help pay the bills to keep the school going. She could tell you about running a before- and after-school daycare for all of the kids in the school so that the parents who couldn't afford the hundred dollars a month tuition could qualify for the daycare subsidy and pay for both the school and childcare out of that. Ask her about eventually going to the local school board and successfully asking for her one room school to be adopted by the school district and funded publicly.

And now during the pandemic, ask her about having her grandchildren come to her house two days a week to play with her, and explore the world, because they are starting from scratch again and running a home learners cooperative. Eighteen children and their families use the ministry of education funding through a distributed learning teacher who facilitates two days a week of in-person learning. The parents organize a three-days a week childcare cooperative with themselves, grandparents, and friends.

There are and always has been global and local communities of people who are actively engaged in this alternative (to) school movement. You are not alone. Children do learn. They do not require institutions.

Be the community you want your child to grow up in.

Changing the Context

By Antonio Buehler

"Hello, Kenton," I said to the eleven-year-old seated across from me on the floor. He sat slouched over, avoiding eye contact, staring at the shoe on his extended leg, seemingly a warning to not to get too close.[1] I asked him why he was interested in joining our education community. He did not have an answer, but he was eager to share that he had "really bad teachers" at his prior school. "No one took the time to listen to me," he added.

After a long pause I asked him what he likes to think about. "Robots," he answered. "I had an idea about why robots will take over. Humans can't contain emotions." He added that Star Trek was not a perfect human society because "humans have a lot of problems." When I asked what could lead to an improved society, he raised social justice issues. He was most concerned about police brutality and colonization, and he wanted to learn more about those issues at Abrome.

◆

At Abrome, the Self-Directed Education community where I spend my days, we have limited time to build relationships with young people. We reject the designation of school, just as we reject most of the practices and structures of schooling; but similar to school, we are a place where young people spend six hours a day, for about 180 days a year, for up to thirteen years. That's a lot of

---

1   This essay is a work of nonfiction. Names, genders, and some descriptive details have been altered to protect the privacy of individuals.

time, particularly if someone is forced to spend it where they don't want to be, yet it is only about 20 percent of their waking hours in a given year.

Families who seek us out tend to fall into one of two camps. The first camp consists of those who are running toward us, most often with a focus on finding a liberatory environment where young people can practice freedom on a daily basis. It is with the young people in this camp that we often have the luxury of time, as they tend to stay with the community long term.

The second consists of those who are running away from something that has deeply harmed their children, although sometimes they are just hoping to stop the compounding violence of schooling that amplifies other forms of trauma. This camp tends to be more focused on emancipation from a harmful institution. In large part, we are seen as a trauma center for families that have run out of options. But we want to do more than just stop the bleeding; we want to assist healing. Too often though, when the bleeding stops, with comfort knowing that the worst is behind them, the family moves on, sometimes reintroducing their kids into the same environments they were running from in the first place.

Without the certainty or luxury of time, but freed from the constraints of trying to shape young people into some idealized adult vision of what they are to become, we focus on changing the context instead of changing the individual. Changing the context is the quickest and easiest way to support young people no matter the level of distress in their lives.

Opt out

I met Barb and her fifteen-year-old son, Devin, at the local coffee shop. I introduced myself to Devin, but he just stared at the table in front of him. Barb explained that Devin had recently been hospitalized and needed to find an alternative school as soon as possible because of the harm that school was causing him. I turned and asked Devin if he wanted to leave school. Keeping his head down, he said nothing. I told Barb, "he doesn't have to go back to school tomorrow." I explained that finding a new school was secondary in importance to stopping the pain, which she could do by withdrawing him from school immediately. Devin looked up and said, "I would like that."

◆

Dominant culture believes children cannot be trusted to make their own decisions; if left to their own devices, they will derail their futures. Therefore, by way of parenting and schooling, children must be guided into adulthood. Although the manner of parenting (e.g., authoritative, authoritarian) and schooling (e.g., progressive, classical) that is accepted is not uniform, control over children is the narrative that society has internalized, and it has become so entrenched that opting out seems radical.

Baked within the conventional assumptions of what parenting and schooling should be is a belief that children are not capable of understanding what is in their own best interests. These beliefs are too often the justification for ignoring young people's cries for relief or help, which ultimately leads many children to completely withdraw from meaningful engagement with their families and the communities around them.

Individually scrutinized, the generalized beliefs around conventional parenting and schooling can be seen as absurd on their face. Does a child need to be able to sit quietly for long periods of time around adults? No. They could be free to play, so long as guardians are not wedded to the belief that children must be docile. Do they need to learn to read by the age of five? No. They could learn to read when they are ready, so long as they are not placed in environments where they are ranked against same-age peers.

But even when we pick apart the individual arguments, people still revert to a general faith in adults wielding power over young people, arguing that we should just tweak or remove the more absurd practices, instead of recognizing that power over is the root absurdity. The first step to changing the context can be acknowledging that conventional parenting and schooling are nothing more than harmful belief systems that have been conditioned within us, and that opting out is a possibility.

◆

A month later, Barb gave me an update. She took my advice and withdrew Devin from school, allowing him to stay home, and she believed it saved her son's life.

Personal autonomy

Stephanie told me that her autistic child, Zachary, was in a constant state of distress at school, and that he would bring that distress home to the family each afternoon. Stephanie first tried to advocate for accommodations at the local public school, and when that did not work, she enrolled him in the most progressive school she could find. Yet she still found herself physically prying his fingers from the door frame each morning to go to school, and trying to find ways to ameliorate the compounding symptoms of physical illness that seemed to stem from the stress. Zachary felt trapped in environments where he was expected—so adults could feel comfortable—to contain his emotions, ideas, and movements.

◆

When young people are in distress, adults often attempt to help the child manage through it. This rarely benefits the child, as the causes of the distress are usually external. Depending on their identities and places of being, young people can be impacted by the wide variety of social, economic, and legal forms of oppression that adults also face. Other than those who are incarcerated, no group of people are more routinely denied autonomy over their bodies and minds than young people. Autonomy is a basic human need, and distress in response to violations of that autonomy is not a defect of the child. We can change the context for these young people by removing the oppressive practices and structures that are placed upon and inhibit the autonomy of children.

Removing such practices and structures requires self-reflection on the many ways that we, as adults, police young people for the sake of convenience. Whether we head to work while we send kids to school, or we stay home and allow children to roam unschooled, we tend to make decisions for them with our own needs, or the needs of people other than our children, in mind. From an efficiency perspective, this can make all the sense in the world. Young people are more impulsive than adults, and are less likely to abide by social norms, especially social norms that prioritize their docility. If the goal is to minimize social disruption or move everyone along a similar path (e.g., classroom activities) then tolerance for individual deviations from the group quickly wanes. But what makes sense to those with power, in terms of efficiency, can lead to terrible outcomes for individuals, with many historical examples of the worst of outcomes when efficiency over autonomy becomes institutionalized and systematized.

When it comes to culture building within groups, a more nuanced debate about the limits of autonomy may be warranted. In a group, it serves everyone's interest to feel safe, which necessitates that each person consents to being a member, and that agreed-upon boundaries are honored by all. Boundaries often include expectations of, or limitations on, ways of being (e.g., noise level, eye contact, active participation). The challenges for young people are that they do not get to choose their family, they are often placed in communities against their will, and they typically lack the resources needed to navigate out of spaces that violate their autonomy. With this in mind, adults must endeavor to strictly limit any encroachments upon personal autonomy to only those that are necessary for the well-being of a consent-based community, or to protect the autonomy of others. We must scrutinize the many generally accepted expectations of, or limitations on, young people that are unreasonable, such as demands for performance and productive output, controls on movement (e.g., stimming), and notions of respectability. And bodily integrity should be non-negotiable. We must also provide ways for young people to opt out of situations where they perceive their autonomy would be unduly inhibited.

◆

As a result of Stephanie's decision to move Zachary from an environment that disregarded his personal autonomy to one that openly acknowledged it, many of Zachary's struggles quickly disappeared, and the quality of his life and that of his family improved substantially. For example, the tussling each morning at the door disappeared, and Zachary and his family avoided a stressful event at the beginning of the day, which helped head off a cascade of follow-on crises.

Acceptance

After our morning meeting on Gabriel's first day, he asked if he could play video games. I said, "Yes, you get to decide how you spend your time here." Thirty minutes later I was walking through the space and I noticed a cable running from an outlet into a closet. I knocked on the door and heard, "Come in." I opened the door and saw fourteen-year-old Gabriel on his knees playing on a laptop. I asked if everything was alright, and he said it was. I asked if he wanted to interact with others, and he said he preferred remaining in the closet. He stayed there until the end of the day.

Gabriel's routine continued day after day. The other facilitators and I became more and more concerned that perhaps we were not properly supporting someone who chose to wall himself off in a closet for the entire day, every day. Our schoolish lens had us worried about missed opportunities for development, as well as possible questions coming from his mom about how he was spending his time. We chose to push down our insecurities, prioritize being welcoming and inviting, and honor his desire to be by himself.

◆

We live in a society predicated on hierarchy. We judge others (and ourselves) by where they fall within various hierarchies. And where they fall determines, to a large degree, on what access, privileges, and so-called rights they have. The pyramid structure of society requires large numbers to fill out the base, so that a select few can benefit from their place near the apex. In other words, most people have to be labeled "losers" in order to justify the outsized gains of the "winners" in an ostensibly meritocratic society. We see these hierarchies in almost all economic, legal, political, and social institutions. These hierarchies not only determine who benefits and who exists to serve those who benefit, they also perpetuate and reinforce the unjustness of other existent hierarchies (e.g., white supremacy, ableism).

Young people are not immune from the impacts of hierarchy. In fact, hierarchy is a primary force that shapes them. As an oppressed group with negligible economic and political power, they are seen by government and industry as raw material to be molded into reliable workers and consumers (the base), while their family often encourages a climb to the top. Because the aforementioned groups are constantly measuring the youth (e.g., grades, athletic performance, leadership positions) in an attempt to rank and sort them, young people learn quickly how they measure up to their same-aged peers.

Unfortunately, the cloud of competition leads to a denial of self, as their ways of being are scrutinized and used as inputs for placement within hierarchies. While families with sufficient material resources may find ways around it, children who are considered too far below or behind arbitrary behavioral or performance norms are often singled out and treated as defective. Children whose identities are not idealized by dominant society (i.e., those who are Black, Indigenous, trans, undocumented, autistic, etc.) risk amplified marginalization.

Because of the unforgiving nature of the pyramid structure of society, young people must expend significant energy masking their emotions to ward off scrutiny from adults in positions of power. This harms young people in the moment and in the future, as it forces them to ignore their most basic needs, denies them meaningful relationships, and hinders their natural development. Adults can change the context by accepting the child for who they are and their ways of being. Acceptance allows for the emergence of psychologically safe spaces where children are free from assessment, judgment, or ridicule. Instead of declaring what is important and then measuring it, adults can trust kids to take what they need.

◆

The closet door in many ways was a physical boundary that Gabriel used to protect his emotional boundaries, and for perhaps the first time in his life, Gabriel's boundaries were honored. Like many young people who have been wounded both in school and in their personal lives, Gabriel did not need to be pushed into activities or behavior that made adults feel comfortable—he needed to be accepted for who he was in the moment, and to have his needs centered. After a month, Gabriel left the closet for good, and fully embedded himself at the heart of the community.

Question authority

During one of our twice-weekly "Flying Squad" days, we stopped by the Texas State Capitol. Flying Squads is an intentional effort to support young people in reoccupying public space in our anti-child society. The young people I was with chose to explore the grounds, and twenty minutes later Kenton and Harriet came back to tell me that they had been kicked out of the visitors' center. I asked why and they said because they were without a chaperone.

◆

Children are oppressed in contemporary society, in part, because many ostensibly well-intentioned adults believe oppressive practices are necessary to prepare children for an unfair world. This is shortsighted on two accounts: First, oppressing children doesn't better prepare them for future oppression. Abuse wears people down, forcing them to expend limited personal resources trying to minimize, resist, or escape it. Second, oppressing children seeds future oppression. It is easier for people who have internalized the oppression of one group (i.e., children) to rationalize harming others (the houseless, BIPOC, etc.) or supporting institutions that do (capitalism, white supremacy, etc.). And simply having been oppressed in the past is not automatically some form of inoculation against being willing to accept the oppression of others, particularly when people get to graduate into the class of the oppressor (i.e., adulthood). Adults can instead engage in the struggle of youth liberation.

Youth liberation compels us to change how we interact with kids, but it also requires that we go further by using our relative privilege to alter the ways that other people and institutions interact with young people. One of the most powerful methods of doing so is to question authority. We must start by critically examining whether forms of authority are ethical, how that authority is established (or imposed), and how authority is perpetuated. Then, we need to identify ways to subversively challenge that authority.

When we interrupt child oppression, young people see that we stand in solidarity with them. We change the context. We let them know that, though we are free from the age-based discrimination they face, we are still concerned with their struggle. We let them know that their experiences and their lives matter to us. And that recognition can open up conversations about how liberations are intertwined, how none of us are free until all of us are free, and how we can support the liberation of others. In this way we not only stand up for them—and children everywhere—we seed in them the capacity to stand up for others.

◆

When I walked into the visitors center with the young people in tow, a member of the staff and a security guard met me at the main desk. I asked why they'd kicked the young people out of the center. With the young people listening intently, I wanted to model how we can question authority. The staff member said they were worried about kids being in the building without an adult. I told them that we believe that young people have as much of a right to navigate public space as adults do.

Their supervisor then joined us at the desk and stated that it was policy that children have a chaperone with them. When I asked to view their policies, she told me that it was not written down as a policy, but it was instead a commonly enforced practice. I pointed out that, since it was not a policy, they did not have any right to restrict these kids from being able to roam unaccompanied through the center. The supervisor then asked who would be held liable if the kids injured themselves or damaged something. I said I would be. I then turned toward the young people and told them to enjoy themselves. Kenton's eyes met mine while I was saying that, and he smiled. Then Makayla, recognizing that everyone was still standing around, said, "Alrighty," and off they ran.

Place within society

I looked out the window and saw Kenton, Leo, and Raj playing in the grass about fifty yards away. Then I saw seven-year-old Leo, who was visiting as a prospective member of the community, throw a large rock into the road. I walked outside to have Leo remove the rock from the road and to bring everyone back to Abrome. I turned to Kenton, who was a few years older than the others, and said, "We need to take care of each other." He replied, "I'm not a babysitter."

I asked Kenton, who had only been with us for a couple of months, if he felt he had any obligations to others. Kenton changed the subject and said that he was upset because this was supposed to be an "activist school" and that he didn't feel as though we were doing enough in the community. I responded that we were trying to create something that went beyond protesting or getting arrested. I explained that we were trying to live prefiguratively—meaning we were trying to organize and engage with each other in ways that not only allowed us to navigate and improve the society we live in, but to model the relations that a better future society would entail.

◆

Why should young people believe that this world is for them? They can't vote, even though the consequences of political decisions will most often impact them more than any other age group, as they are the ones stuck with laws and policies the longest (because older generations die off). In sick societies that value wealth accumulation over collective well-being, this leaves younger and future generations with the burden of reckoning with legacies of human rights violations, dispossession, poverty, and environmental degradation.

Young people also have limited control over their own bodies. Thanks to compulsory schooling laws and testing, kids are situated in environments where they are forced to compete against peers on measures that often have no meaning to them, and are subjected to punitive rules that regulate everything from what they can wear to when they can talk. The lack of bodily autonomy also extends beyond the schoolhouse. They are age-limited on employment options, and the number of hours they can work "when school is in session." At home, even in cases where young people are being abused, states prohibit children from emancipating themselves until their mid- to late teens, and then only if they are self-supporting, which is an impossibility for most because of the restrictions placed on youth employment. Even in the most supportive homes, kids are unable to access certain types of healthcare (birth control and vaccines, for example) without permission from parents or guardians.

While youth liberation can seem like a fantastic delusion at times—especially to young people—we can help youth reconceive their place within society, and support them in acting on society, so that they can take ownership of changing the context of their lives and of the world around them. We may not be able to liberate them by ourselves, but it can be liberating for them to realize that we trust them to not only make decisions about how they spend their time and what their education looks like, but also to engage with the world in order to alter it. Being able to live what we want to create in the world can be the most liberating feeling of all.

◆

Two weeks later, we dedicated our tri-weekly field trip day to supporting the houseless community, spurred primarily by a vicious public backlash by right-wing groups to the Austin City Council decriminalizing houselessness. The decision was a personal one for one of the kids, who had been houseless the year before. We made hundreds of lunches and a large pot of soup, and went to three houseless encampments in the city to distribute the food. Many of the young people got into extended conversations with the houseless folks, particularly Kenton, Harriet, and Olivia. The experience allowed them to feel as though they could take action to materially improve the lives of people beyond themselves.

Moving on

Kenton had joined us in the fall of 2019, hoping to put an end to a string of bad schooling experiences. While I was shocked by how he had been treated at his prior schools, it was learning about the trauma he faced in his personal life that really floored me. That trauma helped explain many of his initial difficulties: defensiveness, angry outbursts, an unwillingness to trust others, and dissociation when stressed. But, by changing the context in all the ways mentioned in this essay, over the span of about half a year, he slowly learned to trust us, trust in himself, and trust that he could improve the world around him. Unfortunately, once the pandemic hit in 2020, he had to move out of state to be closer to family.

◆

Changing the context has an outsized (arguably the greatest) impact on the quality and direction of the lives of young people. Parents and guardians have about eighteen years to support children, while caregivers and educators have far less time. While we can lament the years children may have needlessly suffered through the expectations and limitations of dominant society, today will always be the best day to change the context.

Listen To Children

By Sara Zacuto

Since shifting my role from being a classroom teacher to becoming the parent educator here at my school, my role in facilitating project work with the children has diminished.[1] It's something I truly miss, because learning alongside four- and five-year-olds is lively, engaging, enlightening, and challenging. But a while back I was inspired to begin a project all on my own. It started with a simple desire to share meaningful quotes with our community of parents and educators who would tour our school occasionally. I wanted to post these quotes in our classroom environment as provocations for dialogue, and also to provide accessible talking points that promote critical thinking about child development and the importance of play. I printed candid photos of the children and included a relevant thought or idea from the wealth of great thinkers I know of and admire. People like Janet Lansbury, Bev Bos, Alfie Kohn, Heather Shumaker, Loris Malaguzzi, Fred Rogers, and many, many more.

After I'd made and hung a few up, it became evident that this was a powerful way to frame the learning that was going on every day in our school. It became a simple way to document the children and show people the purposeful, productive, and enriching play and work that was happening in every corner of our school. I wanted people to look with new eyes at pictures of the children running, digging, pouring water, or climbing, and gain a deeper understanding of what was really happening for the children in every photo.

---

1   Sara Zacuto, "Listen to Children," *Little Owl School Blog*, March 26, 2018, https://littleowlcommunity.wordpress.com/2018/03/26/listen-to-children.   Adapted with permission.

They weren't "just playing."

They were putting in the meaningful social work of forming new relationships, taking physical and emotional risks, solving problems, testing boundaries, imagining, hypothesizing, figuring out how things operated, building, deconstructing, creating, moving their bodies in novel ways, engaging their senses, thinking, feeling, constructing knowledge, and a million, million other things.

There are always going to be people who doubt that children are capable of learning without being "taught." There are always going to be people who look for proof, or some sort of product to take home at the end of a day that ensures *something* was learned. This, I think, is the result of various factors, including fear-based societal and cultural pressures, a deep and systemic flaw that promotes testing kids relentlessly (because knowledge *must* be measured or it doesn't exist!), well-intentioned, competitive parents who unwittingly pit their children against others (even though I believe they feel like they want their child to "succeed"). These are just a few examples of the simple misunderstanding of what children really need. What they really need is *trust*.

It is hard to step back and trust young children, because it requires relinquishing control. It requires us to let go of *our* desired outcomes, of the idea that *our* expectations should be met, and instead that we focus on the child's expectations. It feels nearly impossible. This boils down to trusting children, and not just their capabilities. It's easier to trust that a child is learning when they are active, motivated, and busy, but trusting them even when they appear to be doing *nothing*? That's hard! Trusting that they might be in a period of reflection, taking things in, thinking, observing, or really needing to be accepted as an introvert is something we are not socially conditioned to do.

Trusting children became the message that was ringing loudest in all the quotes I was drawn to. The more quotes I gathered, the more it became clear that they needed to be compiled into a book, which would feature a photo of every child in our school. It would carry the strong message to *trust their learning*. After a couple months, I had completed it. It is a collection of pictures and ideas that promote an image of children as capable, trustworthy, self-driven learners. It's what I absolutely believe about them, and want to shout from the mountaintops.

As with every project I've worked on, I wanted to get input from the children, hear their ideas, and include their voices. I decided that because our annual art auction was coming up, creating a canvas with the children featuring a relevant quote would be a perfect contribution. I grappled with which excerpt to choose. I thought it had to be simple, eloquent, and profound. I wanted it to encapsulate the very essence of childhood ... a tall order. I figured I would present a few to the kids and let them choose which one stood out to them. A few quotes resonated with me, until (ding! and duh!) TRUST CHILDREN! Even I forget sometimes, or need to challenge myself to trust even *more*.

What would they put on a canvas?

What do they have to say?

What is the idea they want to put across?

I came up with the right question to present to them: "What do you want grown-ups to know about children?" The conversation was actually quite brief. The very first idea came about when a child said, "You should listen to kids, and do the stuff they want to do," and another chimed in with "Listen to them when they talk to you." So, after reflecting their words back to them, it became simply, "Listen to children."

The next idea came just as quickly, when I felt a tug on my shirt and bent down to the child who was not feeling brave enough to announce her idea to everyone. When I heard the secret that was being whispered in my ear—"Let them laugh and play"—I don't know if it was the whispering, or the idea itself, but shivers went down my spine when I heard it.

LISTEN TO CHILDREN. LET THEM LAUGH AND PLAY.

It was perfect.

We began to work on the large canvas, drawing intersecting lines, and a bubble in the center to contain the children's words. I knew that I wanted them to print out their idea themselves, with me only helping them to spell. Besides being utterly charming, I find children's early writing to be especially poignant and powerful, and I also wanted this piece to belong to them as much as possible. Once the words were written out, we began filling the canvas with a lovely palette of forest green, blushy pink, pale yellow, and shimmery bronze. Everyone in our classroom contributed to it, and over the course of a week it was finished.

Due to time constraints, I felt that the question I originally posed to them wasn't entirely answered. I wanted to give them the opportunity to explore their thoughts on the subject even more. So I brought the question to our afternoon gathering to continue reflecting as a group and hear about what all the children believed about their rights in our world. And since there were so many more ideas and no more room on our big canvas, we decided to make another little one expanding on the topic about what grown-ups should "let" kids do. The kids, of course, had lots (!) to say.

Listen up grown-ups! This is what our children want us to know! This is what they want for themselves. They want to dance, jump, climb, and skip! They want to draw and play, kick soccer balls and make books! To put on their own shoes and say *poop*! Paint, sew, get messy, dig, and hug!

They want to run free, and do nothing … to solve problems and smell roses! They want to know they can do anything. They want to be heard.

And they want to be trusted.

A Fatigue-Wearing Judas: Acknowledging Histories and Breaking Cycles

By chris time steele

"We all need histories that no history book can tell, but they are not in the classroom—not the history classrooms, anyway. They are in the lessons we learn at home, in poetry and childhood games, in what is left of history when we close the history books with their verifiable facts."
—Michel-Rolph Trouillot, *Silencing the Past: Power and the Production of History*

The teacher rolled the TV cart into the room. The cliché squeaky wheel was all that could be heard as we were herded into the library at my high school. Silence, the smell of a smuggled Jolly Rancher, uneasiness, innocent chuckles that mask anxiety shallowly echoed. My history teacher, Mr. Lynch, who assigned us Jesus as required reading, who wore cowboy boots with jeans and a polo, bean pole thin. He looked like a cartoonist from Nickelodeon drew him, animating him as he paced around the library with his bushy mustache. Mr. Lynch said, "Today is a day you all will remember, a day that will go down in history."

It was 2001, September 11th. No context, we watched the news, the TV replaying the planes smashing into the Twin Towers over and over again, three thousand lives lost, a million more were set to be murdered as the propaganda wheels churned. Kids ask questions, kids have intuition, kids have answers, and find answers. One of the questions being asked was, "Why do they hate us?" The common and ridiculous gaslighting answer was "because of our freedom."

Playing basketball that evening, the skies were eerie, devoid of airplanes, North Denver's thin air was thick with tension.

Listening to hip-hop was essential while playing basketball in the alley. My older brother first introduced me to hip-hop when I was five; he had an NWA tape and put it in when our parents left. He said, "Don't repeat anything you hear on this," which enticed me to memorize every line.

I never considered Mr. Lynch a teacher, I considered him an authority figure who wanted to control, not to educate. I had my real teachers; KRS-ONE,

Chuck D, MC Lyte, Dead Prez, Ras Kass, Yasiin Bey, Common, and Talib Kweli. KRS-ONE taught me about police violence and the CIA (Criminals in Action). Chuck D taught me about the power of solidarity and the history of Martin Luther King Jr. Day. MC Lyte's "Poor Georgie" taught me about relationships and the dangers of drinking and driving. Dead Prez taught me about Fred Hampton, nurturing the body with plants, the Black Panthers, and Nat Turner. On the song "Sharpshooters," M-1 from Dead Prez mentions Nat Turner. I asked my teacher who that was and he said, "It's nonsense, there never was such a person." Luckily, I never trusted Mr. Lynch, so I went to the library and asked the librarian who looked up Nat Turner and his rebellion and led me to some books.

Ras Kass's song "The Nature of the Threat" opened my eyes to the legacy of white supremacy, the suppression of history and the meaning of "Western Civilization means white domination."[1] This song made me reflect on being a settler, having a colonized mind, and my role in the structures of violence. Yasiin Bey taught me about the power of water and control. Bey's song "Mathematics" broke down the statistics of white supremacy, explaining unemployment, the wage gap, and the prison industrial complex. Common taught me about Assata Shakur and her importance in fighting against white supremacy and imperialism. One of the most important songs for me during the time was "The Proud" by Talib Kweli. This song came out in 2002, a little over a year after 9/11. It helped take the fragmented feelings I had and put them in order, it solidified my resistance and empowered me. This song broke through the propaganda and actually gave context to 9/11, explaining how the US empire had intervened in the Middle East for decades. Hip hop gave me permission and the power to say "No" when, following 9/11, Mr. Lynch told me to "be a man" and would repeatedly try to give me pep talks about joining and fighting for my country when the military pulled their Hummers up to Westminster High School and took over our school.

In our P.E. class, the military came in and tried to hype us up. The recruiters dressed in fatigues, made us do pushups, and praised me, telling me I was strong even when I started shaking at twenty pushups. They played basketball with us and told us about the good games at the military and said they'd help us get on a college team. Women recruiters were flirtatious, they offered to take us to lunch in the Hummers. My friends and I went many times for the free food; they would take us to get fast food on our lunch breaks, complimenting us, feeding us poison, asking us to sign papers. Years later I reflected

1 Ras Kass, "Nature of the Threat," track 5 on *Soul on Ice*, Priority Records, 1996, CD.

and called it a psychic draft, but it was much more personal and coercive than that, it was grooming, predatory grooming.[2]

I have no illusions about why some join the military. Our high school was a working-class school. College recruiters did not line the hallways; school counselors laughed at me when I said I wanted to go to NYU. Due to expensive healthcare, ever increasing college tuition, and stagnant wages in the US, many find themselves economically coerced into joining the military. Howard Zinn explains that there is no evidence that humans have "a natural instinct for war. If that were so, we would find a spontaneous rush to war by masses of people. What we find is something very different: we find that governments must make enormous efforts to mobilize populations for war."[3]

Along with hip-hop, luckily, I had my mother. She is loving, she is fierce, for better or worse she doesn't hold back how she feels. My mother was an oncology nurse, she often worked night shifts, fourteen-hour days. My mom told me to never sign the recruiters' papers and that there was no use for war, that she'd take her kids to Canada before letting the military have us. In a disorientating time, full of paranoia, fear, and angry talks of revenge and war, her strength was comforting.

Along with PE, the military took over our history classes. "Wanted" signs for Osama bin Laden went up. I was so conditioned to tuning out Mr. Lynch that I didn't listen much to the military recruiter cosplaying a teacher. I remember Mr. Lynch pulling the boys in our class aside and telling us that it was our duty to go, that we could be heroes if we caught Osama bin Laden. While Laura Bush was speaking about "severe repression" against women in Afghanistan, we weren't told that the Soviets had used the same argument when invading Afghanistan in 1979.[4] We weren't told that Reagan dedicated a space shuttle flight in 1982 to Afghan freedom fighters when they were called "anti-Soviet insurgents."[5] We never learned about the Revolutionary Association of the Women of Afghanistan (RAWA) who were advocating for themselves before

---

2   Amy Hagopian and Kathy Barker, "Should We End Military Recruiting in High Schools as a Matter of Child Protection and Public Health?," *American Journal of Public Health* 101, no. 1 (January 2011): 19–23, https://www.ncbi.nlm.nih.gov/pmc/articles/PMC3000735.

3   Howard Zinn, *A Power Governments Cannot Suppress* (San Francisco: City Lights, 2006), 190.

4   Kim Berry, "The Symbolic Use of Afghan Women in the War on Terror," *Humboldt Journal of Social Relations* 27, no. 2 (January 2003): 137–60.

5   Reuters, "Space Shuttle's Flight Dedicated to Afghans," *New York Times*, March 11, 1982.

the Soviets invaded; they resisted the Taliban and the US.[6] If I was taught this history... I'm not sure if I would have heard it, but the cycle could have been disrupted. Even more important, learning is about unlearning, relearning, or learning-through as well. "Unthinking a chimera," unlearning settler narratives, an ideology that has been cemented as history through years of propaganda.[7] Hip-hop was an intervention into these narratives, and meeting compassionate artists along the way opened my mind and nurtured me through shared solidarity. Unlearning isn't an event, it's an ongoing process, which involves being in community with others, reflecting on internalized white supremacy, and diagnosing the patriarchy within myself.

My high school was in Denver, the homelands of the Cheyenne and Arapaho. A settler colonial city built on a foundation of violence and extraction. Our high school mascot was a "warrior," a racist Indigenous appropriation. The war machine was reproducing itself once again with another war. Osama bin Laden's CIA code name was Geronimo, an Apache who fought against US colonialism. During the Iraq invasion in 2003, the military referred to Iraq as "Indian Country" to "designate enemy territory."[8] Indigenous historian Roxanne Dunbar-Ortiz points out the military "identifies its killing machines and operations with such names as UH-IB/C Iroquois, OH-58D Kiowa, OV-1 Mohawk, OH-6 Cayuse, AH-64 Apache, S-58/H-34 Choctaw, UH-60 Black Hawk, Thunderbird, and Rolling Thunder. The last of these is the military name given to relentless carpet-bombing of Vietnam peasants in the mid-1960s."[9] Michel-Rolph Trouillot frames the conversation of historical production hauntingly well: "We imagine the lives under the mortar, but how do we recognize the end of a bottomless silence?"[10]

I think back to my elementary and middle-school classes where we were assigned to write letters back to our imagined families in Spain because we were so-called explorers on Christopher Columbus's ships of genocide.

---

6   "Revolutionary Association of the Women of Afghanistan Struggles Against the Taliban and The U.S.-Funded Northern Alliance," *Democracy Now*, October 4, 2001, https://www.democracynow.org/2001/10/4/revolutionary_association_of_the_women_of.

7   Michel-Rolph Trouillot, *Silencing the Past: Power and the Production of History* (Boston: Beacon Press, 2015), 72.

8   Roxanne Dunbar-Ortiz, *An Indigenous Peoples' History of the United States* (Boston: Beacon Press, 2014), 56.

9   Ibid.

10 Trouillot, *Silencing the Past*, 30.

Another activity involved us writing in calligraphy on paper grocery bags from the Mayflower, telling of our harrowing journey. We were taught nothing of the violence the settlers inflicted on the Indigenous. The teacher came by with a lighter to burn the edges of our letters to make them look old, symbolic of the torching of truth and perspective that we would never learn. Thinking back to Mr. Lynch, his required readings of Jesus, his cowboy boots, settler colonialism, white supremacy... it reproduces itself. James Baldwin diagnosed the cycles of ideology and history remarkably: "The great force of history comes from the fact that we carry it within us, are unconsciously controlled by it in many ways, and history is literally present in all that we do."[11]

Context matters, embracing curiosity matters. With the foundation of my mother's strength and with hip-hop music, I was able to fight the disorientation of the war machine's propaganda. Hip-hop gave me a political vocabulary, a foundation to US settler colonialism, and a critical history that helped me see cracks in the narrative of the mainstream media. Nas's song "What Goes Around" spoke about how Indigenous folk helped saved the pilgrim and in return the pilgrims killed them, exposing Thanksgiving for what it truly represented, not a holiday but a "hell-day."[12]

Like most kids wracked with anxiety, I hid in the school library. I ended up becoming a volunteer there. Diane, the woman who worked in the library, listened to my interest in hip-hop and asked what the songs were about, much different than being in the classroom.

Diane tracked down a book about Nat Turner, she found *The Autobiography of Malcolm X*, and some books about hip-hop's history from the Black Spades to the Zulu Nation, and she embraced my curiosity. I had been rapping through high school as well but felt insecure and inadequate. The librarian read my lyrics for a song I later released called "Universal Battle." She loved the song, she encouraged me, she was a support structure in an environment that was seeking to regiment kids to support an imperial structure.

My friend Anthony was a point guard on our basketball team. A Chicano, always with a smile, he could handle the ball and had a devastating crossover. We lost touch after graduation. I saw him years later at a bar on Broadway in Denver. I spotted him in a crowd; the brain can do amazing things like that by recognizing familiar faces. I swayed through people to reach him and when he turned around, I noticed he was missing his left arm from the elbow down. He greeted me, still smiling. There was a familiar

---

11   James Baldwin, "The White Man's Guilt," *Ebony* 20, no. 10 (1965): 47–48.

12   Nas, "What Goes Around," track 13 on *Stillmatic*, Columbia Records, 2001, CD.

silence though, a silence that he shared with some of my family members who were drafted to Vietnam. They don't talk about war either. He said he could still break my ankles though with a crossover, we laughed. My smile decayed when I walked away. I later found out that he went into the Army after high school and lost his arm and part of his leg after hitting a roadside bomb. We were just kids; why did the military come into our school after 9/11? Why did the teachers let it happen? Why did we let it happen? Would he have gone if they didn't come? I worried about what wars were still going on in his head and what trauma he was dealing with.

It's been just over twenty years since 9/11. Ripples of my decisions from high school continue to echo. From wearing a Talib Kweli shirt in health class I met my friend A.C. who told me his cousin made beats. His cousin turned out to be the producer AwareNess, who is still my best friend. We've been making music since then and have traveled the world, a different type of tour, making music finding communities through art. In order to survive while making music, I've been a custodian, a pot washer, a dock worker, I've driven a snow plow, been a mover, worked in a library, was a journalist, a teacher, a truck driver, and worked in a call center. Hip-hop always taught me the value of reaching out, finding mentors, collaborating and coming together. It was my friend Sole, a hip-hop artist, who told me to reach out to Noam Chomsky, which led to a friendship and being part of one of his books.[13] Friends and elders have told me harsh truths with loving kindness, and educated me on the violence I perpetuated with my words and presence in some situations. Through the ongoing cycle of learning, unlearning, and relistening, I hear the homophobia and patriarchy in songs I used to admire. Some of my former heroes are under scrutiny for harm they've caused. Through listening and reflecting, I've grown, and undoubtedly have much more growing to do and many more chimeras to unthink.

I had trouble writing this story. Writing isn't always hard, not hating yourself is hard. Saying "no" is hard and explaining that *no* can be draining. Writing your story and your truth can be disillusioning, but when you do, you realize you aren't as alone as the process of writing can feel. Back to basketball, when you write, the ball, the narrative is in your court. The narrative of white supremacist capitalist patriarchy has been written in blood in this country for 530 years. A cycle that keeps reproducing itself, a settler stealing land, hoarding resources; a recruiter walking into a school, searching for young hearts to taint

---

13   Noam Chomsky, *Occupy: Reflections on Class War, Rebellion, and Solidarity* (New York: Zuccotti Park Press, 2013).

with darkness in a Conradian fashion, then give them back to their families, a heart changed, now purple.

Breaking cycles can be important. Disrupting whiteness, gender norms, colonial narratives, breaking down hierarchies. The importance of sharing stories and deplatforming authority is exemplified in the following quote by Trouillot: "History does not belong only to its narrators, professional or amateur. While some of us debate what history is or was, others take it in their own hands."[14] My mother's firm *no* to joining the military. The librarian who read my songs and found books outside of my high school's required readings. Hip-hop music that wasn't played on the radio, which spoke a poetic truth and dreams of liberation. These are all examples of cycles being broken, opening new worlds.

Below is the song I shared with Diane (the adult who worked in the library).

Lyrics to Universal Battle, featuring Amber, 2003
By Time (produced by AwareNess, guitar by Ricardo Cruz)

Long ago, the universal battle took place, between the sun and the moon
Why must we fight
[Amber:] Why must we fight
If we join together, we'll shine bright
Why must we fight
[Sun:] You ain't nothing just the reflection of my light and power
My rays shine bright
Against the cold I offer protection
I evaporate the rain after showers
My position in the heavens determines your hours
I'm the sun god Commonsense praised me
It wasn't the big bang theory
The all mighty god raised me
In the west I rest towards the east I rise
My heat dries the tears from your cries
Theories stating that all planets don't revolve around me
Are nothing more than lies

---

14   Trouillot, *Silencing the Past*, 153.

If the earth's axis shifted a mile closer to me, mankind would reach its demise
I shine so bright no mortal can look me in my eyes
[Moon:] Now wait, hold up
You know different from all the other stars in the sky
Acting like you special cause you waste light on human civilization
For me they built space stations and rockets
Little do they know, I hold alien life forms in my meteor craters and pockets
[Sun:] Man, because of my gravitational pull your humans is standing
[Moon:] For me they televised the first space landing
[Sun:] Come on
Who do these women with no self-confidence go to when they need tanning?
[Moon:] I'll be here forever
Blessed by Jehovah
Your running out of time before you red giant and super nova
I was searching for peace, trying to hide the innocent
While you were shedding light over wars
Bullets being tossed, death, battles and the holocaust
Watching my people get crucified on the cross
Constellations shine with me to guide the lost
Vampires prowl under my light
Tao monks meditate in front of candles they write
Werewolves howl under me when I'm full
I raise the tides, over gravity I have control
Claiming you hot, but I can't feel you in the winter
Three out of four seasons
You omnipotent? Give me one more reason
I'm the beacon of light in the darkness never leaving
You got the homeless dying and freezing
I offer no damaging sun rays, killing people with cancer
Nocturnal animals worship me
I camouflage the panther
If I question the people of darkness
It's me, to whom they answer
[Amber:] Why must we fight
If we join together, we'll shine bright
Why must we fight
[Sun:] I'm the sun you son
S-U-N you the S-O-N
My solar flares corrupt the technology of men

You appear in quarter half and crescent, I'm always full
I shine on all borders, feel my wrath
Brighter then fluorescent my light has soul
Third world countries could take you out with one missile
Your light's artificial, meteors don't affect me
Your surface is riddled with craters
You miniature to me, a piece of candy, you wanna battle now or later
I'm more respected, add it up the math agrees
Phoenix, named their basketball team after me
The light you emit is so dim, that humans had to develop candles
Who was responsible
For melting Icarus's wings and sandals?
Crime occurs at night time you responsible for schemes and sandals
You got no color, I offer rainbows plus my sky is blue
You're nothing new, this solar system alone got forty of you
[Moon:] You retreat after half a day
I'm here to protect it
So why should a coward be respected
Thinking you're powerful
Coppertone'd you down, humans merely use sun screen
Thinking you a god?
We all came from one being
I show the big dipper and reveal constellations
All you offer is clouds
People think they see figures in the sky but it's just patience
Mixed with imagination
I am the man on the moon
Physical features is fact a true person you're facing
Saying you make change
But your revolutions go in complete circles
What are you chasing?
[Sun:] Nine planets revolve around me
You're just a rock following the rest
Shadows fade when I peak over the horizon
Even if you had a number two pencil you couldn't test
I am the day, you just a knight, I'm the king
The center of attention
Mother nature's my queen
I'm a real rock

When they take me for granted I burn these human beings
You're weak
A pacifist
I've never seen moon screen
[Moon:] You get your light taken out with a simple eclipse
[Sun:] I am Ra, praises of Arabic, spit, drips from Egyptian's lips
[Moon:] Under my constellations, ancient pharaohs lined up their pyramid tips
Rest in peace sun or should I say R.I.P.S
[Sun:] You're insignificant
In the book of the universe
You wouldn't even get a caption on a page
[Moon:] You're forgotten, your assassination wise elders is plotting
Where were you during the ice age?
[Amber:] All of this fighting is worthless
All of life deserves a purpose
Why do we fight, let's shine
[God:] All bow, this is god, time and space
For too long I watched these humans fight over land, religion and race
I'm the distance in between all this war and battling
I'm the only reason you two are here
I know all and see all
I'm the wind that guides the whisper to the ear
The universe is one
All is connected
Everybody got their own reason
It's karma you should be respecting
Sun, you guide the people and give them light
You feed nature down to the roots your impact is deep
Moon, you hide the innocent, giving people peace to sleep
I gave you Sunday and Monday, you both are equal
There's billions of moons and stars in this universe
If you let hate and envy overcome your emotions there won't be sequel
There's been much too much, blood on my name, nothing is worthless
When will we learn that both light and darkness serve a purpose?

Abolish High School

By Rebecca Solnit

I didn't go to high school. This I think of as one of my proudest accomplishments and one of my greatest escapes, because everyone who grows up in the United States goes to high school. It's such an inevitable experience that people often mishear me and think I dropped out.[1]

I was a withdrawn, bookish kid all through elementary school, but the difficulty of being a misfit intensified when I started seventh grade. As I left campus at the end of my first day, people shouted insults that ensured I knew my clothes didn't cut it. Then there was P.E., where I had to don a horrendous turquoise-striped polyester garment that looked like a baby's onesie and follow orders to run or jump or play ball—which is hard to do when you're deeply withdrawn—after which I had to get naked, in all my late-bloomer puniness, and take showers in front of strangers. In science class we were graded on crafting notebooks with many colors of pen; in home economics, which was only for girls—boys had shop—we learned to make a new kind of cake by combining pudding mix with cake mix; even in English class I can remember reading only one book: Dickens's flattest novel, *Hard Times*. At least the old history teacher in the plaid mohair sweaters let me doze in the front row, so long as I knew the answers when asked.

In junior high, everything became a little more dangerous. Most of my peers seemed to be learning the elaborate dance between the sexes, sometimes

---

1   This essay was published originally in *Harper's Magazine* as an "Easy Chair" column, and has been slightly updated here. Rebecca Solnit, "Abolish High School," *Harper's Magazine* (April 2015), https://harpers.org/archive/2015/04/abolish-high-school.

literally, at school dances I never dreamed of attending, or in the form of the routines through which girls with pompoms ritually celebrated boys whose own role in that rite consisted of slamming into one another on the field.

I skipped my last year of traditional junior high school, detouring for ninth and tenth grades, into a newly created alternative junior high. (The existing alternative high school only took eleventh and twelfth graders.) The district used this new school as a dumping ground for its most insubordinate kids, so I shared two adjoining classrooms with hard-partying teenage girls who dated adult drug dealers, boys who reeked of pot smoke, and other misfits like me. The wild kids impressed me because, unlike the timorous high achievers I'd often been grouped with at the mainstream school, they seemed fearless and free, skeptical about the systems around them.

There were only a few dozen students, and the adults treated us like colleagues. There was friendship and mild scorn, but little cruelty, nothing that pitted us against one another or humiliated us, no violence, no clearly inculcated hierarchy. I didn't gain much conventional knowledge, but I read voraciously and had good conversations. You can learn a lot that way. Besides, I hadn't been gaining much in regular school either.

I was ravenous to learn. I'd waited for years for a proper chance at it, and the high school in my town didn't seem like a place where I was going to get it. I passed the G.E.D. test at fifteen, started community college the following fall, and transferred after two semesters to a four-year college, where I began, at last, to get an education commensurate with my appetite.

What was it, I sometimes wonder, that I was supposed to have learned in the years of high school that I avoided? High school is often considered a definitive American experience in two senses: an experience that nearly everyone shares, and one that can define who you are, for better or worse, for the rest of your life. I'm grateful I escaped the particular definition that high school would have imposed on me, and I wish everyone else who suffered could have escaped it, too.

For a long time I've thought that high school should be abolished. I don't mean that people in their teens should not be educated at public expense. The question is what they are educated in. An abolitionist proposal should begin by acknowledging all the excellent schools and teachers and educations out there; the people who have a pleasant, useful time in high school; and the changes being wrought in the nature of secondary education today. It should also recognize the tremendous variety of schools, including charter and magnet schools in the public system and the private schools—religious, single-sex, military, and prep—that about 10 percent of American students attend, in which the values and pedagogical systems may be radically different. But despite the caveats and anomalies, the good schools and the students who thrive (or at least survive) high school is hell for too many Americans. If this is so, I wonder why people should be automatically consigned to it.

In 2010, Dan Savage began the "It Gets Better Project," which has gathered and posted video testimonials from gay and lesbian adults and queer-positive supporters (tens of thousands of them, eventually, including professional sports stars and the president) to address the rash of suicides by young queer people. The testimonials reassure teenagers that there is life after high school, that before long they'll be able to be who they are without persecution—able to find love, able to live with dignity, and able to get through each day without facing intense harassment. It's a worthy project, but it implicitly accepts that non-straight kids must spend their formative years passing through a homophobic gauntlet before arriving at a less hostile adult world. Why should they have to wait?

Suicide is the third leading cause of death for teens, responsible for some 4,600 deaths per year. Federal studies report that for every suicide there are at least a hundred attempts—nearly half a million a year. Eight percent of high school students have attempted to kill themselves, and 16 percent have considered trying. That's a lot of people crying out for something to change.

We tend to think that adolescence is inherently ridden with angst, but much of the misery comes from the cruelty of one's peers. Twenty-eight percent of public school students and 21 percent of private school students report being bullied, and though inner-city kids are routinely portrayed in the press as menaces, the highest levels of bullying are reported among white kids and in nonurban areas. Victims of bullying are, according to a Yale study, somewhere between two and nine times more likely to attempt suicide. Why should children be confined to institutions in which these experiences are so common?

Antibullying programs have proliferated to such an extent that even the Southern Poverty Law Center has gotten involved, as though high school had joined its list of hate groups. An educational video produced by the S.P.L.C. focuses on the case of Jamie Nabozny, who successfully sued the administrators of his small-town Wisconsin school district for doing nothing to stop—and sometimes even blaming him for—the years of persecution he had suffered, including an attack that ruptured his spleen. As Catherine A. Lugg, an education scholar specializing in public school issues, later wrote, "The Nabozny case clearly illustrates the public school's historic power as the *enforcer* of expected norms regarding gender, heteronormativity, and homophobia."

I once heard Helena Norberg-Hodge, an economic analyst and linguist who studies the impact of globalization on nonindustrialized societies, say that generational segregation was one of the worst kinds of segregation in the United States. The remark made a lasting impression: that segregation was what I escaped all those years ago. My first friends were much older than I was, and then a little older; these days they are all ages. We think it's natural to sort children into single-year age cohorts and then process them like Fords on an assembly line, but that may be a reflection of the industrialization that long ago sent parents to work away from their children for several hours every day.

Since the 1970s, Norberg-Hodge has been visiting the northern Indian region of Ladakh. When she first arrived, such age segregation was unknown there. "Now children are split into different age groups at school," Norberg-Hodge has written. "This sort of leveling has a very destructive effect. By artificially creating social units in which everyone is the same age, the ability of children to help and to learn from each other is greatly reduced." Such units automatically create the conditions for competition, pressuring children to be as good as their peers. "In a group of ten children of quite different ages," Norberg-Hodge argues, "there will naturally be much more cooperation than in a group of ten twelve-year-olds."

When you are a teenager, your peers judge you by exacting and narrow criteria. But those going through the same life experiences at the same time often have little to teach one another about life. Most of us are safer in our youth in mixed-age groups, and the more time we spend outside our age cohort, the broader our sense of self. It's not just that adults and children are good for adolescents. The reverse is also true. The freshness, inquisitiveness, and fierce idealism of a wide-awake teenager can be exhilarating, just as the stony apathy of a shut-down teenager can be dismal.

A teenager can act very differently outside his or her peer group than inside it. A large majority of hate crimes and gang rapes are committed by groups of boys and young men, and studies suggest that the perpetrators are more concerned with impressing one another and conforming to their group's codes than with actual hatred toward outsiders. Attempts to address this issue usually focus on changing the social values to which such groups adhere, but dispersing or diluting these groups seems worth consideration, too.

High school in America is too often a place where one learns to conform or take punishment—and conformity is itself a kind of punishment, one that can flatten out your soul or estrange you from it.

High school, particularly the suburban and small-town varieties, can seem a parade of clichés, so much so that it's easy to believe that jockocracies (a term used to describe Columbine High School at the time of the 1999 massacre), girls' rivalries, punitive regimes of conformity and so forth, are anachronistic or unreal, the stuff of bad movies. Then another story reminds us that people are still imprisoned in these clichés. The day I wrote this, news came that, yet again, high school football players were charged with raping a fellow student. This time it's five boys in Florida. In a 2012 sexual-assault case in Steubenville, Ohio, one of the football players accused of the crime texted a friend that he wasn't worried about the consequences because his football coach "took care of it." The victim received death threats for daring to speak up against popular boys, as did a fourteen-year-old in Missouri named Daisy Coleman, who, in the same year, reported being raped by a popular football player named Matt who was three years her senior.

Coleman, who had attempted suicide multiple times (and succeeded in 2020, may she rest in peace), wrote:

When I went to a dance competition I saw a girl there who was wearing a T-shirt she made. It read: matt 1, daisy 0. Matt's family was very powerful in the state of Missouri and he was also a very popular football player in my town, but I still couldn't believe it when I was told the charges were dropped. Everyone had told us how strong the case was—including a cell phone video of the rape which showed me incoherent. All records have been sealed in the case, and I was told the video wasn't found. My brother told me it was passed around school.

I wonder what pieces we'd have to pull away to demolish the system that worked so hard to destroy Coleman.

But abolishing high school would not just benefit those who are at the bottom of its hierarchies. Part of the shared legacy of high school is bemused stories about people who were treated as demigods at seventeen and never recovered. A doctor I hang out with tells me that former classmates who were more socially successful in high school than he was seem baffled that he, a quiet youth who made little impression, could be more professionally successful, as though the qualities that made them popular should have effortlessly floated them through life. It's easy to laugh, but there is a real human cost. What happens to people who are taught to believe in a teenage greatness that is based on achievements unlikely to matter in later life?

Abolishing high school could mean many things. It could mean compressing the time teenagers have to sort out their hierarchies and pillory outsiders, by turning schools into minimalist places in which people only study and learn. All the elaborate rites of dances and games could take place under other auspices. (Many Europeans and Asians I've spoken to went to classes each day and then left school to do other things with other people, forgoing the elaborate excess of extracurricular activities that is found at American schools.) It could mean schools in which age segregation is not so strict, where a twelve-year-old might mentor a seven-year-old and be mentored by a seventeen-year-old; schools in which internships, apprenticeships, and other programs would let older students transition into the adult world before senior year. (Again, there are plenty of precedents from around the world.)

Or it could mean something yet unimagined. I've learned from doctors that you don't have to have a cure before you make a diagnosis. Talk of abolishing high school is just my way of wondering whether so many teenagers have to suffer so much. How much of that suffering is built into a system that is, however ubiquitous, not inevitable? "Every time I drive past a high school, I can feel the oppression. I can feel all those trapped souls who just want to be outside," a woman recalling her own experience wrote to me recently. "I always say aloud, 'You poor souls.'"

Stardreaming

By Curiousism Cyphers

> "To pay attention, this is our endless and proper work."
> —Mary Oliver, "Yes! No!"

Business put home in a guillotine, pulled the blade and named it school
Shop class blues, they put the rivets through you, the classroom turned 180 degrees
Teachers became bosses, classrooms became factory floors, the principal became a warden with keys
Busy work textbook time thieves, we reject those who teach us to kill our darlings and dreams

Edgewalker's deeds created passion paths to share their love letters on
Glittered with rage, their borderless words took flight
Bringing messages to remind us all that we are, who we have always been
The familiar patterns emerge, we pick them up one by one, remembering we connect
Them to constellations below and to the left
Refiguring we prefigure and send out invitations across the generations

We were born scientists, all babies are
We don't need to be bussed into an institution to learn about the stars
We learn from the smell of willows, not asbestos tile and shushes that echo off moldy baseboards
We learn from being outside, from serviceberries, from oaks, and acorns
Inspiration runs dry on erase boards, is it any wonder they outline dead bodies and also teach with chalk?

We are co-learning our way to liberated futures, autonomy flowering as we
   walk
We are roots underschools, under patriarchal homes, under empires, unbuilding foundations, unbuilding walls
Grounded futures, mycelial webs, learning to love, making mistakes, learning
   to fall

He kōrero

By Jon Pawson (Ngāti Porou/Pākehā)

Ko Hikurangi te maunga. Ko Waiapu te awa. Ko Ngāti Porou te iwi. Ko Jon tōku ingoa.
Hikurangi is the mountain. Waiapu is the river. Ngāti Porou is the tribe. My name is Jon.

I am a parent. To me, that's a virtue of the highest order, a responsibility I've been fortunate to be bestowed with, a role I take seriously and one of the central most parts of my identity. I also have anxiety; I've had it since I was a child and pulled single strands of hair out of my head, one at a time, until I had a number of bald spots. So it goes without saying that parenting is something I think about all the time. I worry about it. I second guess myself. I overthink it. Add another part of my identity to that mix—anarchist—and there's another lens with which to view and question myself and my relationship with my children. Are we done yet? No way! I am Māori, a disconnected one (as so many of us are), having been raised away from and without a firm link to my tūrangawaewae in Tokomaru Bay on the East Coast of Aotearoa.

We can leave the identity markers (crises?) there and see that parenting isn't a smooth path to skip down while happily humming to oneself. It is a political and cultural landscape, fraught with any number of obstacles and challenges for those of us looking to take the road less traveled. Family, friends, community, society at large, all ready to offer you unsolicited words of advice, which are frequently thinly veiled words of criticism. But it has made all the difference that those lenses through which I view the world have led me and my partner to make decisions that we, as a whānau, continue to benefit from: the acquisition of te reo Māori (the Māori language) and a connection to te ao Māori (the Māori world) being the biggest of these. But this isn't about me really; it's about my relationship with my kids and what that looks like. Let's have a wee kōrero about it. I've got two children, T and N. T's almost thirteen as I write this; he's about a month shy of becoming a teenager. N's just had his ninth birthday. They're great kids, kind, and inquisitive. They've got beautiful natures and get on well together. I'm constantly thankful for them and the way they've impacted my life. There's five of us in our household: myself, my partner Kez, our boys, and our doggo Frankie. Kez and I are both working parents, our boys both go to public/state schools, though they've both been in the bilingual streams since they started. Frankie's an arsehole but he's lovely when he's not barking at invisible interlopers or scratching at our legs.

Regardless of your cultural heritage, our tīpuna left us a great many wisdoms in a number of forms. For me, as a Māori, I find great wisdom and inspiration in what are known as pepeha or whakataukī, proverbs that impart teachings to us in a succinct form. When I think about whakataukī and the way these inspire me, I also think about my children and the ways that they have inspired me, the teachings they too have imparted. It's a really comforting thing to be surrounded by this wisdom and inspiration that comes from these two different directions: one from my tīpuna, offering sage advice from times past, but also from my children who inspire and teach me without really being aware of it.

That's one of the most important things I've learned from being a parent, raising and relating to T and N. I don't own them, our relationship isn't transactional, and they don't owe me anything. I get as much (if not more) from them as I give, and there's no tally kept in this regard anyway. Young people aren't formless putty to be molded in ways the adults in their lives deem worthwhile. Through their journeys and explorations in the world, they have as much to teach us as we do them. But you never really understand this unless you take the time to kōrero with them. Kōrero isn't a lecture with a speaker and listener, one active, the other passive. I think society sees the parent-child relationship as a one-way flow with the information and teaching going from adult to child. Kōrero is a relationship of sharing. It goes both ways. There's a really important whakataukī that attests to this.

He aha te kai a te rangatira? He kōrero.
What is the food of the chief? It is kōrero.

Food is nourishing. We need it to thrive. Conversation and discussion are like the most delectable kai to taste and savor. I get a real buzz after conversing with someone, sharing thoughts and ideas, and learning. I notice a definite change in my mood and mindset when I haven't had a solid kōrero in a while. Because we've always held space for kōrero, our boys are always up for it.

I like to think that by valuing kōrero and giving it a place of primacy within our whare, we're modeling to them that conversation matters. Things are better said aloud and discussed than left unsaid to fester. That's a hard lesson to action in my life outside of our whare; there's plenty I want to say to whānau and friends, relationships to be repaired and worked on, but much of the time I lack the courage and energy to go about doing it. But in this whare, we speak to each other. Nothing's off-limits and we discuss most anything in a way that T and N can understand. In doing so, involving our kids in kōrero, I believe we're showing them that the things they have to say are valued as much as Kez and mine are.

The upshot of this is that T and N are forthright with their thoughts and opinions. A lot of the time they don't need to be prompted to share what's on their minds. Silly, serious, thoughtful stuff all has a place in our whare. I trust that this will continue on into their teenage years and beyond because of the groundwork we've laid together in making space for and prioritizing kōrero.

Ko te rātā te rākau i takahia e te moa.
The rata was the tree trampled by the moa.

Another reason we prioritize kōrero in our whare is that we don't want things that T and N see and hear in the media, school, and wider whānau and society to be taken as truth without having the opportunity to talk about it. The whakataukī above speaks to the lasting effect that damage done to a child can have, and it imparts that we be mindful of what's happening in and around our kids. Just as a tree that is trampled as a sapling won't grow upright afterwards, we try to be mindful that the things they experience now will have profound effects upon them as they grow.

Raising our boys in ways that perpetuate the harms of capitalism, misogyny, and colonialist society isn't ever going to allow them freedom. If we were to just go with the flow 100 percent of the time, we'd be doing them a life-long, soul-deep harm that might never be resolved. Racists and right-wing scumbags raise their kids to believe hateful crap, weighing them down with baggage that might never be shed. Why not instill values of love, connection, kindness, generosity, solidarity, whanaungatanga, manaakitanga, kotahitanga? If we do our best to end the generational trauma we've experienced and not pass down those harms to our boys, that's the greatest act of love and solidarity we can give them.

Kōrero is an important tool in exposing conditioned thinking that might sometimes come out in the ways we speak and act around and toward each other. By keeping those channels open, we can discuss things that happen *when* they happen. Owning our words and actions, and being able to apologize to each other for them, has been an important lesson for our whānau.

Being able to explain why we're apologizing and what might be wrong about something we've said or the way we've said it allows us further kōrero about how those words or actions may have come about. I've observed that adults don't seem to apologize to children very often. The ways that we kōrero with each other and what that looks and sounds like can reinforce any number of oppressive attitudes that T and N might have experienced at school, in other people's homes, on the marae, or in the media they consume, so being mindful of it and willing to confront and kōrero about it is a good way to ensure those attitudes aren't normalized.

E kore au e ngaro, he kākano i ruia mai i Rangiātea.
I will never be lost for I am a seed sown from Rangiātea.
This whakataukī references that we as Māori can never truly be lost because, like a seed, we all have potential within us tracing all the way back to our ancient origins. Whakapapa links us, and through whakapapa we can access that potential. With that grounding in our whakapapa, we have a place from which to speak. If one is lucky enough to be firm in their Māoritanga, it feels much easier to kōrero. That's something I'm conscious of with T and N, that they remain linked to te ao Māori and their reo, and feel safe to kōrero. As far as I can tell, the yearning I had and still have to be Māori isn't one they feel, because they know they're Māori. I've not heard either one of my children express thoughts of "not being enough" or needing to do things to be Māori. They just are. That's beautiful. That's deeply vindicating too. Take that, colonizer!

Disconnection is a painful thing. It's something I've been conscious of since I was quite young and it's something I've struggled with in my adult life. My whānau stopped visiting Tokomaru Bay, where my father is from, when I was young. Being white and not going to a Māori "place" or doing Māori "things" left me with a feeling of absence that I didn't know how to address. It's something I was mindful of when Kez and I were deciding which school T would be attending. I am very fortunate that my Pakehā partner was on board with sending our kids into bilingual units at school so they could be surrounded by te reo Māori and a Māori-centered worldview. It was a decision we made as a way to connect them with their Māoritanga, something we didn't feel equipped to give them. This was the way we were going to ensure they got the reo, by learning in it and hearing it spoken every day, again something we couldn't give them. It's been a learning experience we've all enjoyed.

As an anarchist, I feel like my focus should be *un*schooling or *de*schooling or *home*schooling or some kind of other alternative education. However, the schooling my children have been in has given us as a whānau, an avenue back into a culture and language that was denied to my father when he was moved away from our papakāinga as a child. It's not exactly mainstream education, it might even be considered alternative, but it has been in mainstream schools. Had it not been for the bilingual units at school and the wonderful kaiako teaching my children, we wouldn't be in the position we're in now, with two kids very comfortable in their Māori identities, familiar with language and protocol, experienced in kapa haka, being on marae, all those good things we want for our kids in Aotearoa. The bonus is that I've become more comfortable with Māori things, with friendships and relationships that nourish the part of me that desires to be Māori. That's almost solely down to the schools T and N have attended.

Everyone should speak to the young people in their lives more. Value kōrero, discussions, conversations. Make room for it regularly. Pursue it. And if possible, try to rediscover the things in your culture that nourish those conversations and kōrero. However you manage to find your way back into and reconnect with your culture is going to be different than the next person's journey. It's going to be easier or more difficult than you initially thought, but one of the best motivators for doing so is your children and the kids in your life. Everything I've heard, seen, or read says that Indigenous peoples' ways of relating between the young and old is markedly different to the Western way. So, if you're looking for ways to improve your relationships with the young people in your life, to value their mana: decolonize. Our ancestral knowledges offer us a wealth of inspiration in this regard. You just have to make the choice and begin.

Most of us by now have probably seen the memes that say something along the lines, "We are our ancestors' wildest dreams." I used to find that a bit wishy-washy, but I've come to see the truth in it. If my tīpuna felt about their descendants the way I feel about my children (and I'm absolutely sure they did), then we most certainly are their wildest dreams. I have the greatest faith in my children, their generation, and all those to come, that they will do more for each other and the world than we and previous generations have. In order to help that along though, we need to foster and engage them, and one way to do so is kōrero. Me kōrero tātou ki ā tātou tamariki, e hoa mā. We should all speak to our kids, my friends.

A Place for Every Gift

By Tasnim Nathoo

"If we are to achieve a richer culture, rich in contrasting values, we must recognize the whole gamut of human potentialities, and so weave a less arbitrary social fabric, one in which each diverse gift will find a fitting place."

—Margaret Mead

Dear reader,

I am as surprised as anyone to be writing a foreword to the twentieth anniversary edition of *A Field Guide to Small Humans*.[1] In my wildest dreams, I never expected the little tongue-in-cheek book I wrote in the months before the birth of my first son to have found such a wide audience or to have remained relevant over the years.

Many people ask where the idea for the book came from. All I can say is that I wrote it out of a place of sheer terror. When my partner informed me that we were going to be parents, I was overjoyed. For about three minutes. Then I started sweating. I didn't really understand what was happening at first. I thought to myself "Oh, sweating, is that what joy feels like? Cool." Then I realized that it was panic.

I tried to downplay this new feeling of panic as something normal and something that all parents-to-be go through. And I sought out the advice and support of my family, friends, co-workers, neighbors ... a stranger on the subway, an AA group I accidentally stumbled into ... really, anyone who would talk to me. And they were unfailingly kind. I think they could see the signs of someone who was barely keeping it together.

A lot of their advice was, well ... not bad. Encouraging at the very least. "Trust yourself, you're going to be a great dad!" "You'll figure it out." "Listen to yourself." "Kids are the best teachers." "This is a great book." "All you have to do is take it one day at a time." Some folks even went so far as to

---

1   This is a work of fiction by M.B., and *A Field Guide to Small Humans* is not a real book.

suggest that children practically raise themselves and that parents are mostly "guides." Um, okay.

All I did know for sure was that being ruled by fear is a terrible way to raise children. So I sat myself down and said, "Hey! You've been alive for a couple of decades now. Surely you've picked up a few things about teaching and learning and growing and being. Make a list. A nice and orderly list." And so I did. (If I'm being truthful, I actually started this conversation with myself with firm admonishments along the lines of "Stop! You are a pathetic puddle of frantic feelings and muddled thoughts. This is not helping.")

I was surprised to find that I agreed with my first instincts on the topic of childrearing—that so much of what parents and teachers and other adults do comes from a place of fear. And one of the biggest problems with fear is that it constrains the possibilities that we can imagine for our children. And I knew that I didn't want to raise my child in a world of fear.

I also was able to observe, in my somewhat calmer state of mind, that no matter who we are or where we live or the time period we live in, all adults want to cherish, nourish, protect, and treasure their children. They just have some really different ideas of how to go about doing that.

As I continued to make my list, I began to wonder if my views were possibly not even my own. Is it better to have kids who are respectful of their elders, obedient, and well-behaved? Or children who are independent, curious, and self-reliant? Wouldn't the answer to these questions be shaped by my personal politics? Or by virtue of being a human being living in late capitalism?

A Field Guide to Small Humans was born out of this observation and was an answer to the question: "What would an alien need to know to raise a human child?" The book was meant to be reassuring to other parents who were feeling supremely unqualified to raise a child. I also wanted to change the conversation from being all about parents to thinking about how communities and cultures and societies raise children and what our role is in all of this. I wanted to remind us all of the value of coming to the topic of raising children with an open mind and from a position of curiosity and to remember that so much of what we think we know about raising children is shaped by our own upbringing and the values of the society in which we live.

In the years since the book came out, most of the messages I've received were not from other PPs (panicked parents), but instead from children. I laughed when kids told me they had sat their parents down and read the book to them as a way of helping their parents feel better about mistakes and uncertainties and to get over the feeling that they had to be an expert all the time.

Many kids described the book as helping them figure out what they really needed and to challenge many of the limiting ideas that some adults have about children. It helped them learn that they are more capable than they realize and they can handle more choice and responsibility than they are often given and that having less experience and knowledge doesn't mean they aren't capable of great things.

Margaret Mead once said something along the lines of "In the ideal society, there is a place for every gift." For the longest time, I thought she meant that adults have a responsibility to create a world in which every child can pursue their interests, explore different ways of being, and develop their innate skills and abilities. After talking to so many children over the years who feel overwhelmed by missives to "be true to yourself" and "you'll find your unique gifts one day," I think that I might have got it wrong. It's not about creating a world in which kids find their gifts, it's about creating a world in which kids know that *they are the gift* and that they have a place in the world just because they exist.

I hope that *A Field Guide to Small Humans* continues to be helpful to another generation of children and adults as they find their place on this small, sometimes messy, but shining planet of ours.

~ M.B.

A
Field Guide to
Small Humans

On the Last Leg of the Journey: An Interview with Helen Hughes

By carla joy bergman

In thinking about voices—who has voice, who is listened to, and who is left out—I thought of Helen Hughes, my dear friend and one of my most important long-term mentors. To have a voice, you must have a listener. Helen is the person in my life who does this profound listening. She is always curious and open. Helen gave me voice, and I am forever grateful. She has given hundreds of others their voices, too.[1]

In 1971, Helen co-created Windsor House, an alternative K–12 school in North Vancouver. For nearly fifty years, she was the matriarch of this democratically run school-community, which shut its doors in 2019. The number of people who benefited from Helen is impossible to determine: it includes not just students, staff, and families directly involved at Windsor House, but also all who those folks encountered—the ripple effect is immense and truly awe-inspiring.

Here is my conversation with Helen about voice and listening.

carla: Why and how did you get involved in education?

Helen: My parents were teachers, and my home life was secure. I spent my blissful teen years with my dog Topper in the wilds of Mosquito Creek in North Vancouver. I somehow blocked out my schooling—I was very good at seeming to pay attention while being somewhere else entirely. Adulthood came as a rude awakening. Just nineteen, I married, started

---

1   Originally in the anthology, *Radiant Voices*, ed. carla bergman (Victoria: TouchWood Editions, 2019), 31–38, and slightly edited here.

teaching—forty-five students to a class in those days—and tried to learn how to shop, cook, and clean, as well as work full time. I came up short in all categories. That is when my education truly started.

The first thing I learned was to notice what people were actually saying. I learned a lot from my students. When my daughter balked strenuously at going to school in Grade 2, I got together with some other parents and started a school in my house. We knew what we didn't want but had no clear picture of what we *did* want. The school wobbled along—with the fifteen children playing, making use of the many things available to them, while the parents talked endlessly about the philosophy of learning and teaching. We all read every book that came along. Summerhill was our role model. After four years, we could no longer manage privately, so we asked the North Vancouver School District to take us in, which they did. Alternative schools were all the rage in those days. Windsor House, so named because it started in a house on Windsor Road, grew and thrived. Eventually we had two hundred students, and I was made vice principal. My three children attended Windsor House, and now my grandchildren do as well. They are all fine people, so freedom can work if it suits your style.

carla: Helen, you have always been part of educational projects and movements. Can you tell us some of the things you learned most from this work?

Helen: I thought that when I turned seventy-five I would just coast to the end. I'd lived a great life—felt joy, excruciating remorse, grief, a great deal of pleasure, and a lot of just managing from one day to the next. I worked hard and played hard, and now I could take it easy. How wrong I was! There is no rest for the curious, so I am careening down the last run of the rollercoaster—with my hair flying, my eyes wide open, and my ears perked. What I have learned most from this work is that listening to understand is completely different from listening to make a clever rebuttal.

carla: What is next on the horizon for you?

Helen: I decided to spend what is possibly the last fifteen years of my life finding out who I am. I discovered, of course, that I keep changing, so I never really get a handle on it. Also, since I am so embedded in my culture, it's hard to know what is the essence of me and what is the result of conditioning. I'm still curious about it but no longer see it as something I can actually complete. So now I'm hankering for one last project—something that I can manage, something simple, something where I won't be letting people down as I become more doddering and forgetful.

carla: I love that distinction of being part of culture—to know where you start and where the culture ends is challenging for any of us. Do you have any ideas on what that next project might be?

Helen: Well, what are my strengths? I don't cook worth a damn, nor clean, nor garden, nor exercise, nor shop. Hmm. What I enjoy and what I do well is observe people and listen, in order to understand. As a result of this, I notice patterns. One of these patterns is that when people are in conflict and when they start to try to reason with each other, they often use reasons as weapons. They just keep coming up with reasons and counter reasons, and eventually the strongest, richest, loudest person wins, leaving the other person resentful. I rarely see someone say, "Oh, I see your point! Of course, you are right. Let's do it your way."

Reasons are so seductive, though. Check out this link, watch this video, read this quote—then surely, you will agree with me! This popular person, brilliant thinker, renowned scientist says this, so it must be true. It is very unusual to come across someone who is willing to set aside reasons in order to come to mutually agreeable solutions. I am of the opinion that there must be something better.

carla: I agree—there has got to be a better way! I really like the idea of not using reason this way. Can you provide some examples?

Helen: My life's work has made it possible for me to have many young friends, and I noticed that, among the young people that I hang out with, brainstorming seems more effective than sweet reason. The explanation for this is that it is hard for most humans to actually listen to another person's reasoning because half of their brain is busy coming up with a rebuttal. If you are brainstorming, however—just throwing out ideas with no need to favor any particular one—then you can actually hear a suggestion that might appeal to you. Or you hear a suggestion that would work with a minor tweak. At that point, you are both on the same team, trying to create a solution that is good enough to try. Each suggestion should start with words like: "I have an idea," "My suggestion is," "How about we try," "Could we." All suggestions are okay. If you don't like one, then just ignore it. When you hear one you sort of like, then you can add to it with improvements. For older folk, it is much the same: suggestions only, no negation of suggestions, no suggestions of reason or fairness, just possible ideas. The tentative solution need not be bulletproof; it just has to be worth trying. I have an example from today: My grandchildren arrived in a squabbling mood. I intervened. I said that if they were going to be on each other's nerves I would put them in different rooms while I got lunch, and then we could do something together. They clearly didn't want to be separated, so they both chimed in with good will. The eldest had built a fort in the living room and had used two giant padded boppers as door posts. He didn't want his sister to play in his fort. The youngest suggested that they share the boppers. The eldest said no. I reminded them that the best brainstorming is without negation. If they don't like a suggestion, just ignore it. The next suggestion was for the eldest to carry on in his fort and the youngest to help with lunch—then, in quick succession:

- Hop around the house on one foot;
- Cooperate in the fort;
- Eldest play in the fort and youngest have candies; All make lunch together;
- Eldest get the living room and youngest eat grapes while I make lunch;
- Make lunch with feet tied together including me—I had a good laugh at this one, which raised the goodwill of the brainstorming;
- Eldest get the living room and the dining room and youngest get playroom and study;
- Play separately in the same room without bugging; make a fire in the fireplace and watch it.

Unfortunately, the word "watch" sounded a bit like wash, so the eldest said if we wash the fire, then it will go out. He was attempting humor, but it seemed like a put-down, so the energy dropped. I commended the joke and noted that the energy had dropped. Then I suggested one outside and one inside. The energy was wobbling, and we were all hungry, so I resorted to a bulletproof idea that one could use my iPad and the other my iPhone. The eldest picked that up, but the youngest was, to my amazement, unmoved. I was getting hungry myself, so I went back to an old suggestion with a new twist. I suggested that we all make lunch together, but we could walk only on the green squares of the kitchen tiles. By then they were ready to settle. The suggestion by the youngest—that the eldest run up and down the stairs while she counted— was enthusiastically agreed upon. Go figure!

carla: Why do you think it works?

Helen: I am puzzled by the apparent success of this rather odd method and wonder if it can be put to greater use. I recognize that some matters are actually life or death and that running up and down the stairs is not going to help. However, I do believe that, in all disputes, things are either going to stay the same or they are going to change. Given that truism, it seems like a good idea to employ a style that is wide open and without judgments to at least find temporary solutions and, at best, make incremental changes to keep things from becoming too rigid to survive changing conditions.

carla: This model gives voice and power to everyone involved. I think you have an incredible ability to remain curious and to trust both the people around you and the process. How did you learn these skills? Why is listening so important?

Helen: Back in the day when I was fostering young people, we had ample opportunity to try out some of these ideas. My favorite story was about one young person who always left the teapot dirty. When I went to use it, I had to wash it first. We tried this system then that system, but all of them failed. Finally, in a burst of brilliance, my boarder said, "Why don't we both not wash the pot when we are finished with it. Then we only need to wash it just before we use it." I was dumbfounded. My stance was so righteous and hers was so clearly wrong that it took a few moments while I processed the idea and realized it could work really well! Sure enough, when I washed the pot before I used it, the pot was warm as well as clean. When I tell this story to a group of adults, they are often shocked. Some absolutely will not agree that it was a good solution. Somehow it offends a deep moral obligation to always clean up after yourself! This idea of right or fair gets in the way a lot.

carla: What else gets in the way of people being able to approach decisions this way?

Helen: When I was at Hollyhock this summer, they had just issued a ruling that the hot tubs were no longer bathing suit optional. There was grumbling. I said to one gentleman, "Why don't you ask if you can work out a solution with them?" "How could you do that?" he asked. "Either you're naked or you're not—there is no compromise possible." I was astonished, "There are many different options—have different hours for different dress codes; have one hot tub optional and the other bathing suits required; build a screen between the two pools; wear blindfolds; make a tent to put over one; have days on and days off; have times for different sexes, different ages, different moral codes; turn off all the lighting." He was unmoved. I realize that my worldview includes casting about for unusual solutions for seemingly intractable problems. I don't see things as either this or that. I see the world as a place of outrageously improbable solutions that astoundingly work.

carla: Yes, I often say what about options three, four, five, and six? I am pretty sure I gained the ability to ask these questions from being around you. I like what you are saying here. It feels deeply relational, and it makes me think about collaboration. How does collaboration fit into this model?

Helen: Well, it's an informal method of collaboration and can be done by almost anyone. When children have been supported to be successful using informal collaboration, they can do it easily and quickly by themselves in their day-to-day lives. More formal collaboration, however, can only be done by people of good will. It is only effective when meetings are run by a person who can hold everyone to an agreement. The agreement needs to be one of only coming up with ideas, with no spoken or physically indicated rejection. When the felt sense of the meeting moves the moderator to ask if all can agree to try a solution, there may be tweaking of the favorite suggestion to make it acceptable to all. Then comes raised hands to show agreement to support the solution for a given length of time.

I notice that I have used the word *only* three times in one paragraph. I am wary of using absolutes, so I am open to revisiting this.

carla: How do you see this in relation to the question of radical social change?

Helen: I remember being told that in any grouping—people, villages, algae—there had to be about 80 percent of the entities that stayed the same down through time and 20 percent that changed. This was to keep the organism from becoming too rigid to accommodate changing conditions or from becoming too flexible to hold together. This idea made me much more appreciative of all of the rigid systems that hinder the implementation of my wild fancies. Nonetheless, I am very grateful for those folks who get out there and insist on change. You are the ones who get squished and maligned, but you are the ones who will save the day.

carla: If you had one piece of advice to give to those of us who want to see social change in the world, what would it be?

Helen: My advice would be to support one another. If the group you are in heads in a direction you don't want to go, leave. Find a more compatible group or start one of your own. Do not put sand in the gears of a machine that is working. In my lifetime, I have seen many worthwhile groups implode while fighting with one another over insignificant details. Oddly enough, this seems to be a more left-wing issue than a right-wing one. The Right seems more capable of coming up with simplistic ideologies that tap into visceral support, while the Left seems to want to fine-tune to perfection before going into action. When you find a group that you like, appreciate the work of others in your group, use goodwill to understand different ideas, turn criticisms into suggestions, and don't break into secret groups. If you think someone should do something differently, then model how effective your method is. Move toward the trouble—it rarely goes away on its own. Talk with the person you understand the least and listen closely so that you can explain their position with grace. I want to be clear that I do not oppose militancy. There are some groups that need to be stopped. The KKK comes to mind. I'll leave it to you young people to find ingenious ways to fight intolerance and greed.

Creating a Web of Intergenerational Trust

Conversations in Two Parts: in conversation with Wakaba Mine and Joanna Motoi, By Maya Motoi, Japan, 2021

What follows is an exploration of the messiness of what it means to trust each other, and especially to trust children. In both conversations, we aim to animate how this kind of trust is often complicated and not black and white. I also wanted to portray this dynamic by keeping some of the contracting aspects in these conversations, and not polish it to make perfect "sense," because I don't think there is sense to it—it's everything all at once. It's innate and we are all part of cultures of mistrust, but there are also aspects of trust within that, too. This all becomes entangled in our relationships, which means it's nonlinear. So, there is not an official end to these conversations because these stories are relationships in motion.

I was born in Osaka, Japan, in 1993—to my mother Joanna Motoi, who is Canadian-born to Dutch immigrant parents and had been living and working in Osaka teaching English, mainly to children. My father is Japanese and was born and raised in Kobe, coming to live and work in Osaka as an adult. We lived in Osaka until I was about five at which time we moved to the countryside (rural Kyoto prefecture). I did a mix of not going to school, attending some regular school, and also attended Katsuyama Children's Village (an alternative school located in Fukui prefecture). When I was thirteen, I went to Canada alone where I attended Windsor House School, a publicly funded democratic school in North Vancouver, BC. After I stopped going to Windsor House, I was involved at the Purple Thistle Centre (a youth-run arts and activism space in Vancouver). By nineteen years of age I moved back to Japan where I lived and worked for a year in Osaka, and then moved to Kyoto city.

Part One: A Conversation with Wakaba

When I first moved to Kyoto city in 2014, I knew almost no one, but after a month, through a friend of a friend, I met Wakaba. At the time Wakaba was parenting S who was about fifteen, and they also lived with one elderly cat. Our mutual friend, who was also part of the parenting-group talks had also been told to look up Wakaba when she got to Kyoto, and first met Wakaba because S had a stall where she was selling crow feathers and rocks, at just seven years of age.

My first meeting with Wakaba was at a Setsubun[1] party at their place. The second time was at a birthday picnic, which all the people who were co-parenting had organized for S. They had put together a skit of S's then-favorite anime.

Wakaba is always feeding everyone delicious food, baking everyone a birthday cake, organizing things such as sex education discussions for parents with young kids, and doing child care. A few years back, they had also set up a time each week where they would invite us all over to their place to play with a then nine-year-old kid who lived close by with just one parent. Or, when S was going to manga/anime school, Wakaba would rent a room in the (sort of) community center and would invite anyone else that might be interested to practice drawing each other. Wakaba is always willing and engaged with difficult and important community conversations, and talking about how we can better have them together. Wakaba is always inviting people into their journeys of healing, growth, and learning. I am always astounded by their generosity.

My conversation with Wakaba took place on May 29, 2021, and was translated from Japanese from my notes.

Wakaba: On this subject of trusting children, the important thing is: what enables parents to trust children? And how supported are the parents? And how much support is there from the community? Perhaps the rest is the parent/community's beliefs, like believing in more democratic relationships. Of course it becomes dogmatic if these things are simply an ideology.

Maya: In what way do you think parents need to be supported?

---

1   Setsubun is a celebration of the arrival of spring (Chinese New Year). There are various facets of how it has come to be celebrated including aspects I take some issue with, as well as commercialization etc., but this is all beside the point of this piece so I will not digress.

Wakaba: Well, we should ask: are the parents isolated? Do they have people they can ask for child care? How many people is the child directly connected to (without that connection being through another adult)? If that child wants to see that person, can they meet them or get in touch with them by themself? When we were having the child care meetings, one of the kids who was part of the meetings would make phone calls to adults living close by to ask them for their own child care. However, I do think that person to person connection is still a small sphere of connection and that what we need is whole neighborhoods to be connected. For example, in a certain area of Kyoto, even children younger than school age are able to go and play alone when they feel like it. There are kids who go over to a neighbor's place at 7am and kids who are on walks alone after dark. I think it's wonderful that these things can happen. But I do think that there are very few places where these sorts of things are possible. It is difficult to change the neighborhood that you are living in but some people are doing so one small step at a time.

Maya: I feel like people idealize the old days where people played outside and the whole Nagaya[2] life sort of thing... I mean people grew up oppressed in that environment too, and are oppressing other people now...

Wakaba: Well, I guess it is not just about the environment but philosophy as well... I think I just said that I thought it was mostly about the environment with the rest of it being the beliefs of the parents and community, but I think it might be layers of environment and beliefs.

There needs to be situations where there is dialogue in the home and in the community. I think that there have to be places for adults to learn. I think that having a living community and the practice of self-organizing means that we can constantly be renewing ourselves.

When channels of communication are opened up, adults can say things like, for example, "The other day in the bath, so and so was pressing his penis up against his younger sister and I didn't know what to do about it."

And we can have conversations in the community about physical boundaries and the adults can start to be able to talk about these things without being nervous about it.

---

2   Nagaya is inexpensive single story row housing in cities. When the Nagaya life is being referred to, people are usually talking about how there were many people living in close proximity to each other with thin walls, and not much money so there was a situation where you had little privacy and everyone was helping each other out, sharing food and watching each other's kids.

Through community conversations about sex education, adults that didn't know what to tell kids when, for instance, they asked what 69 is, or when they found a box of condoms ... these adults learned how to answer these questions. And it became a positive experience for the children and the adults.

Maya: How did you come to think about this stuff in the first place? What was it like for you growing up?

Wakaba: I grew up during the period of economic growth and our family very much existed as a household supporting capitalism. I grew up in a total void of culture. In the 80s, when I was a child, a TV show called *Toppling of the Blocks* was hugely popular. In that show they depict a child becoming delinquent as a terribly horrific event, which causes the preexisting structure of the nuclear family to crumble away.

To me, culture was *Takarajima* (a subculture magazine) and I found out about punk through it. But we did have our own culture! I just didn't know about it, never had access to it. There is a rich history of the labor movements of coal miners [where Wakaba grew up]. In the mines you would have new labor songs being born every day, but these things were shamed and not considered to be culture.[3] At that time, culture was western things and junk food and drinks. Things like Madonna and Fanta and instant noodles were considered culture. And McDonalds. Imagine ... When the first McDonalds opened there was a line up!

In this environment I felt really lonely and empty and alienated. Everything human was denied. Our lives were not grounded and anything regarded as culture could only be attained through money.

Maya: What were your relationships like with the adults in your life?

Wakaba: Very boring. There was not one adult who I trusted. And because there were no conversations between adults and kids there was no way for us to access their knowledge or different perspectives that they may have coming from their experience. I was only really connected to other kids around my age.

Even though I didn't end up going to university or college, my parents would have paid my way and they fed me. There was financial support, but I had no idea what this world was or how to live in it. I was always being nagged

---

3 Please look up the art of Sakubei Yamamoto (1892–1984) to see his work depicting the life of miners.

by my mom. Not about schoolwork or anything like that but about things like not being able to do what I was told or being lazy or being a slob. She didn't like any kind of weakness. I do think that she felt societal pressure to perform the role that was expected of her as a mother. But there is a limit to this. And I think that her own pain was coming through.

After graduating from high school, Wakaba left home to start attending a cram school in Tokyo in preparation for college entrance, but soon realized they didn't want to go to college so quit the cram school. At this time, Wakaba realized they weren't suited to educational institutions such as colleges, as well as not being suited to living within the perimeters, if you will, set by society at large.

Maya: What was it like when you had your daughter, S?

Wakaba: I was disillusioned with my birth family. At the time that I was pregnant with S, I was dealing with an eating disorder, drinking a lot, and did not have a home. I was either sleeping outside or crashing at someone's place.

I didn't think I could raise a child alone, and I couldn't imagine doing it in a couple. Since I didn't have a home at the time I was thinking about how I could raise a child with the people around me, the people I was already surrounded with in my daily life. But S's father was controlling and didn't agree.

At the time, I was dealing with addiction as well, so I stayed with my parents until S was about three. This was the very opposite of what I had imagined or wanted to do. It was isolating. Then when S and I moved to Kyoto, I started to organize child care meetings. From my involvement with the Kyodohoiku[4] people in Tokyo, I learned about using flyers to gather people[5] and so that's what I did.

After S was born I started sharing my experience of sexual abuse as a child and found that about half of the people I talked to had experienced similar

---

4   *Kyodohoiku* translates to something like "Collective Childcare." Filmmaker Tsuchi Kano explores his childhood of *kyodohoiku* through talking with his biological parents as well as other adults who were in his life, and others raised similarly, in his autobiographical documentary *Chimbotsu Kazoku*. Though it does not have English subtitles, watching the trailer might give you a glimpse: http://chinbotsu.com.

5   I feel that it is worth noting that this is not the first/only example of people handing out flyers to get anyone off the street who cared enough to show up, involved in something as personal as caring for your child. With the movement for independent living of people with physical disabilities, they also handed out flyers to gather people to care for themselves.

things. I learned that a majority of perpetrators of sexual violence toward children are people they know and who they are close to, and I had no idea how to prevent these sorts of things from happening within our child care community. On top of this, all of my energy was used up by dealing with flashbacks from my own experience of sexual violence, and because I couldn't overcome this we couldn't continue the first child care meetings.

After that, I learned about the concept of sex education and also CAP[6] and the idea that children themselves can have power to avoid violence. This had a big impact on me.

The second time I started the child care meetings was when S was about six. I was seeking other adults that S could have not so guarded relationships with—like I had with extended family—homes that were not quite your own but almost like your own home and relationships like that.

Through having meetings at first once a month, eventually the group congealed enough that we didn't have to set up meetings for the group to continue.

Around the time S was nine, she stopped going to school, and it changed from meetings to a group parenting situation. I said to S that I felt that I couldn't be her only guardian and that I wanted to gather other people. What do you think? And S said, well that sounds fine. So I again made flyers, but this time I only gave them to adults already quite involved with S, and she started going to Wakusei.[7]

Maya: When did you find out about Wakusei?

Wakaba: I had actually known about it for a while as I had visited when I was in my twenties. And before S entered grade 1 we had visited, so she did know it was an option, but because of the tuition fee, I didn't exactly recommend it to her at the time.

When S was still going to regular school I remember her coming home in tears because she had only gotten one right on a kanji test. I said, "Isn't it great that you got one right?" But she wouldn't listen and was still upset, so I went to the teacher and explained the situation and asked that they please also applaud S for the one kanji she got right. And the teacher said that they often get the opposite request from parents, to be more strict. The teacher said, "Well, I don't know what I can do since she did only get one right"… It was at this moment that I realized there was no way this school was going to work.

6   Child Assault Prevention is an organization active throughout Japan.

7   Wakusei is a free school in Kyoto: http://www2.gol.com/users/kosa.

I also remember the time that S came home upset about not being good at playing the pianica because a classmate had looked at her strangely when she played. I suggested that we practice together, but when we tried she was so tensed up there was no way we could practice.

And there was also a time when S was telling an adult at our place, "I'm stupid"... The fact that she had already internalized that...

But when S started to go to Wakusei things did become easier and I felt that finally I had the support that I needed. I do think that S was quite empowered by going to there. I remember S telling me stories every day about things that happened at Wakusei.

I can remember almost nothing of going to school myself—only send-off parties when someone would move, and playing musical chairs.

Maya: The only time that I went to a regular school was in grade 2 and that is probably the year of my life that I remember the least about, even though my teacher was a young guy that was into breakdancing, who my family had also befriended. Usually the more experienced teachers are put in charge of the younger grades, especially in a difficult situation where thirty-eight kids from three different schools are being put together for the first time, so even as a child I did feel sorry for our teacher as he often seemed pretty exasperated with us. I remember that when he was at a complete loss about what to do with us he would show us breakdance moves.

Wakaba: Even with a teacher like that there were not many events or things that you remember from that year at school?

Maya: Yeah.

Part Two: A conversation with Joanna Motoi

Some of the underlying beginnings of trust that took hold in my growing up, and in particular my relationship with my parents, is that they believed me. They believed me in everything, whether it was having a headache, wanting to do something, or feeling a certain way. They believed me all the time and therefore I had no reason to mistrust them or really anyone else for that matter.

Just as important, they never belittled me or judged anything I wanted to do, never made fun of it. They fully and sincerely supported me and engaged with my curiosity about the world and whatever project I wanted to do. This support animated my life. When I wanted to raise ducks from eggs or make books, both my parents fully used all their skills and knowledge to support and facilitate me doing these things. What follows is a conversation I had with my mother, Joanna, about all of this, and about raising me.

Maya: I want to talk to you about trusting kids. Not about go to school or don't go to school, but just about trusting kids, and how that can be hard for a lot of adults, even if they believe kids should have more freedom. Though you were looking into some alternative education stuff, weren't you and maybe Dad naturally trusting even before that? How did that come about? I'm sure there are parts of it that you were conscious of but...

Joanna: There had to be because if we just went on the way we were raised, which I think a lot of people do, then there wouldn't have been room for that kind of thing. Coming from a more traditional family, which was pretty strict, the whole idea of trusting your children and giving them the freedom was not part of the picture. There were all these boundaries, and we had the religious side of the upbringing too, so growing up we had to follow a lot of rules and regulations. And we were physically disciplined too. So, wow, where does the trust enter into all that...when you are told to do this, do that, and everything is more black and white, of course not everything was that way ... I will say more later.

So I think when you came along I'd already ... not Moto [nickname for my Dad] ... but I'd already been searching for a different way of being, and I was working with children all along. And this all started from beginning to teach children of a different culture and thinking about how to do it. My very first influence was actually Krishnamerti, the Indian philosopher/thinker. He started schools in India so I was really interested in how he was talking about being with children. That was before you were born, so it didn't come out of the way I was raised. I learned about it through reading. And from him, I went into reading about all kinds of alternatives like A. S. Neill, etc. It was mind boggling in the beginning. So I guess the idea of trusting children was foreign to me, and I had to experience it through teaching kids. Like, oh! It's true, if you trust them, the whole thing blossoms. Everyone relaxes and so much more happens nicely and naturally, and without force and coercion.

And Moto was the same, I think. If it was totally him doing it, he would have raised you the way his parents had raised him, and in Japan, following the whole proper way to be a child. But he trusted me in what I was doing. And it suited him. He said to you and me at one point that he was always trying to get out of the box himself without realizing. So everything he did was a bit rebellious. So he was all for it, including the idea of letting you choose what you wanted to do. He was totally supportive, because he was wanting to get out of the box himself.

Maya: But I guess in Dad's case, like you were saying without reading about the stuff or anything…

Joanna: For him it was just what he was doing with Maya. And he totally trusted me in what I was doing with you. That's an interesting question. So maybe it is in the whole learning and the doing it, the experiential part of it. Since I was trying to change with my students before you were born and then you happened to come along when I was already working on this alternative way of letting kids choose how they're going to learn English.

Maya: You were already on that path, I guess.

Joanna: Yeah, of helping children to grow, sort of. I mean, my small part of it. I wasn't a parent at that time.

Maya: But that seems like a big transition, for anyone I guess, even if you are working with kids, to then have your own kid, because then it's obviously 24/7. The way I remember it, you never told me what to do—not just with big decisions or moments, like going to school or not, but even in everyday things.

Joanna: We made some decisions, like let's go camping this weekend.

Maya: Oh yeah, for things that I wouldn't be able to decide myself or think of myself, you guys made decisions. But in terms of how I used my time, basically. As far back as I can remember I was completely doing whatever I wanted to.

Joanna: How did that happen? Because I don't remember connecting you to what I was doing with the students.

Maya: I guess you wouldn't in a way, because I would have been a baby or toddler and the students would have been older than me.

Joanna: I guess we did trust you but I didn't consciously think: okay, that way of looking at learning is what I'm going to do with Maya. Not at all. I mean I was just busy like: okay breastfeeding; next step, she'll be walking; wow she's not walking yet! So we were just bopping along. We were both really busy, and in your first years you had Yoko looking after you [a mutual friend of my parents who babysat me a lot]. We were sharing you. Way in the back of my mind there was the influence of the whole "it takes a village to raise a child" thing. We didn't feel that we owned you or anything, so it was like, wow Yoko is a mother to Maya too. And we didn't consciously talk about that but that's how we kind of felt. Also, I was in a foreign culture too, so I trusted Yoko to care for you and she was like the Japanese (mother), and also Tani-san [who also babysat me]. Moto took care of you. There was a group of us taking care of you. Catherine [Joanna's friend from Canada] came over when you were first born, so we were trusting others with you too. So it's not just totally about trusting you, the child, but trusting Moto, trusting your partner, and trusting other people in your small community. If you don't trust other people, how can you trust your child? Does that make sense?

Maya: That totally makes sense.

Joanna: But we did trust. In growing up and wanting to get out of my circumstance, to get out of the box, and get to Asia where people thought in a totally different way than the Western world... that was also a freeing feeling. I was also with this Japanese man who knew very little English so we already had to be very flexible and easy in our family to make it go smoothly. And I think that the trust for you to make your choices just sort of came out of that whole thing. It wasn't a "I believe that John Holt says you should do such and such." It wasn't like that. So there were a lot of factors. Me being in a foreign culture trying to raise you, I needed to feel secure that I was doing the right thing, and everything was okay with you.

Moto did whatever, he was so agreeable and supportive.

I said: why does she need to go to school if she doesn't want to? You know we've seen her just learn all these things at home. Moto could understand that, when I'd explain it in that simple way, and he'd totally agree. And so that was that, and we'd never have to talk about it again.

It was like our awakening. It was like, "Wow! She's showing us all the time that she can clearly make the choices for herself. We don't have to force her on a bicycle (for example) like we were forced to learn how to do things."

And it suited Moto. In Japan you are coerced to do a lot—not just go to school, there's a lot more to it in Japanese society, coming out of Confucius thinking, so you have to act in certain ways, and he rebelled about that.

Moto was really trusting. He'd ask, why should my daughter go to the school? And why can't she go off to Canada for nine months? And he could see it was true that if you trust your child, they can grow up in a natural way, which suits their being and their spirit. He could see that, even though he didn't read all the books I read. And that's experiential. Us learning by watching you, our child. That was so amazing.

And it wasn't so conscious that I was like, "Wow! The book is right! We let Maya make her own choice, and look, shit, she's actually at home not just watching TV, she's learning all this stuff! And she wants to know about the moon and the stars!" It wasn't like that. It was just all of us together as a family bopping along and using each other's knowledge. I had the knowledge on alternative education, but Moto had all the technical knowledge, so when you went through the scientific stage... When kids are about nine their interest in science seems to explode. I notice that when I teach the kids now too: usually when they are in grade 4 they suddenly all become interested in science. You were the same, and Dad was great in that way too, you know, to take you off to this star watching thing or whatever, or get the eggs incubated. So you had a good funky combo with me and Dad. And the different cultures gave it more, and we had to be flexible because we were dealing with second-language learning in our home.

So it's not so black and white how it happened, but interestingly there was never doubt. We never thought, "Are we doing the right thing by letting Maya make the choices?" We just wildly thought you should be choosing, so maybe our own realizing carried on to you. As we developed our own learning and little activism for ourselves, we could do it with you.

That was the start of it, and I think that blossomed into not just a trust in education but in life.... It's the same as when you are going through a sadness. You trust that you need those emotions right now, or that alone time or that need to cry. It's not always a cheerful thing, but to trust yourself to balance your own troubles comes is part of it, and that's hard! As a parent, I did want to interfere...

Maya: Like, fix it, or make it better or?

Joanna: Yes, yes.

And that was hard. When you wanted to go to Canada, when you were so young—and you'd been through Katsuyama—there was no hesitation; of course we would support you 100 percent. But, no, the issue wasn't trust; what was it? It was fright. We were scared that something would happen to you. It wasn't about not trusting you to be in Canada on your own, just down right motherly protection/fear that something would happen to you and I was too far away to be able to hug you or comfort you through whatever it was. That was hard.

So, that's a different kind of trust. You wanted to do it, and I had to trust you that you were going to be able to handle every aspect of your experience.

Maya: It must've been hard for you when I first went to Canada because I was having a hard time too. We would talk on skype, and I remember thinking, oh, well at least now we have things like the Internet and free phone calls ... The Internet was too slow at our house for video, so we only had audio.

Joanna: We ended up on the phone.

Maya: When we talked on skype I probably talked about whatever I was going through when I first got there. Because I could only think back on this after, but I did have culture shock, which I didn't expect to have because I can speak English and am familiar enough with the culture, or at least have a knowledge of the culture. But I do think it wasn't just about how it was going at Windsor House, which was part of it, and that kind of sucked. But, I don't know, I'm sure I talked about that stuff with you, but then you're so far away.

Joanna: Yeah, yeah.

So you've just brought up an interesting thing wanting to help you but being too far away; the trust, is not so simple. It's not just about us trusting Maya. We had to expand our trust. We had to trust Yoko with you, totally. So, that can be scary for a parent, especially when you hear of these scary things happening, when you trust the babysitter or whatever and then something awful comes out of it. So we had to expand on our trust so it turns back on us like, are you really a trusting person? You know, theoretically you're doing this with your daughter but now you've let her go, you have to expand your trust to Laurie and James [who I lived with when I went to Canada], my aunt and uncle, Joanna [my cousin], Windsor House, so it's not just trusting that one person, trusting your child, you have to trust that the schooling their going to is meaningful for them, you have to trust that the family they're going to stay with is going to be alright with them, and your trust just has to grow out and out, as they go out, so that was another step. And that was part of the whole thing of trusting Maya, it was like, wait a minute, can I trust this family with Maya?

And then the reciprocal part was trusting that you would be honest, and trusting you to be able to say: "Mom, this family is no good for me." So it's an ongoing thing, the trust.

You brought up something interesting about the letter writing. And I realize it's not all black and white even with my own family. Because as strict and conservative as my family was, they were very free in another way. They were kind of a mixed up family because my mother was raised in a very open and free thinking family... Her mother did Montessori when it was still a totally radical thing from France. She was doing a Montessori school in her home, and my father came from a scary conservative family, raised with Calvinism and the Protestant work ethic instilled in him. But he radically, like your father, wanted out of that oppressive upbringing. So, they trusted me to go to Europe when I was fifteen.

And they trusted us as teens. That's also European. You grow up fast there. Unlike in Asia, by the time you're a preteen in Europe you're able to sit with adults and have a smoke and, in those days, have a glass of wine. Because you're fourteen, they don't consider you a child anymore... Then they trusted you to go off, and get a job. So we did have that kind of trust. We were never told to do our homework. We were totally trusted that we would. And if we didn't it was no big deal. It was just like, oh shit, you didn't do it.

Maya: Well, it's kind of like there are certain strict or very decided things, but then outside of that it's not necessarily so...

Everything is so multifaceted, and like you were talking about with your family, it's rarely just one way completely...

Joanna: I think that influenced me, now that I think about it. That they let me go off so young and do that. I mean in those days... to get on an airplane...

Maya: What year was that?

Joanna: I was fifteen so, early 70s, maybe. And connected to the trust is the whole societal thing of growing up. Like, I think when we were young we grew up faster. By the time you were eighteen you were expected to be sort of acting like an adult, whereas now... and in Japan it is very late. Even at twenty a lot of people are so protected here by the system, the school system, the familial system. I think it must be hard in Japan to transition into adulthood.

Maya: I think so.

Joanna: So, you did that very young… With the Europeans, we felt that whether it was a conservative family or not, you took on the whole societal responsibility at a younger age. So that was carried over into Canada with Opa and Oma, following the European way, so I mean I worked with a lot of other Europeans. Italians were all out working by the time they were sixteen and most people weren't protected. By the time you were fourteen you were looking for work, so that is a kind of trust to grow up and take care of yourself.

It's a societal trust thing and we were bridging two cultures here, so that was nice for you that you could go, and do things like get a job. And that helped with you being able to take care of yourself too. Another very cool way of learning.

Maya: I do feel that, as opposed to growing up in a more conventional Japanese way, I had a lot of opportunities to sort of figure out basic life skills, I guess. Just things like finding and doing different jobs, or finding a place to live, or cooking for myself—a lot of these things that I think are very basic life skills that a lot of people in Japan often don't get to experience until much later…

Joanna: Back to the trusting children. These days I work with children, who are grade 6, preteen. Last year was the first time they were here without their parents and I really felt that thing about trusting kids. I was a bit nervous, I didn't want an accident to happen, but I thought, wait a minute, just trust them. I thought about how they are never trusted, and I gave them the day off, which was a bit difficult. I couldn't do it totally naturally because I wasn't the parent and I was worried. So a different kind of trust. They came here and I trusted them to take care of themselves for the whole day, and entertain themselves. It was beautiful when they were given the freedom to just be sort of mellow and go their own way. And some of them would naturally do it. They didn't have to play together, which is such a Japanese thing, you know you have to do this as a group together, which I think bonded that group. And they're coming again. It's the last time they're coming and that's why I was saying to you and Moto, I just want to be A. S. Neillian all the way and just let these guys do what they want to do, even just for one day, which is them learning to trust themselves. So, you use the word "self-regulation," and that's beautiful, like to self-regulate their mood, how they want to spend their time, how they learn. As children we're not given a lot of freedom about how we want to learn, or how we learn best. So, I'm having to deal with this trusting children all the time.

Not with you anymore, ha ha.

Maya: Well, yeah, ha ha.

Joanna: If it's you now, it's just "oh poor Maya she doesn't trust herself on that one. Ha ha. We're sort of exempt.

Maya: Well, I guess I shouldn't laugh because a lot of people … even if their kids have moved out and are adults are a lot more entangled in their lives…

Joanna: How does it work now that we're finished?

Maya: Finished for a long time.

Joanna: Yeah. So how does the trust work for you now? Switch that from us trusting you, how did, with us trusting you, how did that work for you in taking care of yourself?

Maya: I feel like I can't even conceptualize it.

Joanna: Like, can you trust yourself? Like, to, I don't know, in all situations…? We don't know the outcome, only you do…

Maya: I think I can't quite connect it to how I am, because this goes back to when I was born so it's just how I am. But I do think it connects to the things we've talked about before—like trauma. It relates to the work I am doing now, and how I perceive myself now. I'm not afraid of people, or situations with other people, so I think I basically trust people. I mean not just humans. Other living beings, and I guess beings that are not "living" too. So I think that's probably how it comes out the most for me. But on the reverse side, I feel there is a lot of conflict within me when I feel people being not trusting. Or trying to trust but not being able to, or just offering a kind of conditional trust.

Joanna: I mean everybody's different, right? Sometimes people said: "Well, Maya is so good, what if you had a kid that…" I'd say, well, I don't know, I think I would have had a nervous breakdown or something. So we were just blessed with a very independent person from the beginning. We didn't create you… And I think all humans are born with an instinct to trust. And trust is part of a survival instinct. It's not some beautiful woo woo; it's just survival. I have to trust you because, if I don't, I'm dead.

Sometimes it turns out to be a horror story, but children are born into a family and they have no choice but to trust. And when the trust gets broken, you have trauma. Maybe trust is a need. To trust somebody and if it's reciprocated, that they trust you too, then it can blossom maybe?

Maya: I think so.

Joanna: It's not something you have or not… I think you bring it out in people or not. Or you suppress it. In Japan a lot of kids aren't trusted, and then they're an adult and they have a hard time working while navigating this whole Confucian hierarchy of relationships.

Maya: I think hierarchy is a replacement for trust, right? Because if you have trust you don't need hierarchy, but you can default to the hierarchy even if you don't have the trust. Or even if you don't feel it.

Joanna: Yeah, you have to trust the boss. You're stuck in it. It's false.

Maya: It's a false thing but it's also kind of a tool, I think, to default to in the place of actual trust.

Joanna: Back to what we talked about at the beginning, it was through a lot of study, and being like wow, it's true! But doing so subconsciously maybe? I don't know. By then it was internalized within me and so it flowed with you. It was like: yes, of course trust Maya. Yeah, I had been reading and studying all that before you were born and as you were growing up, so it went together. Internalizing it and seeing it with you. It still blows me away that we are so un-trusting of nature to take care of itself.

When you strip away all the ritual, the child can learn instead of being told things like "god says to be good." That is so bizarre. The idea that "I must be good." Or that you are forced to love your neighbor as yourself. Bizarre. So if you strip away all that societal stuff I think you can naturally respect, maybe that's it? And I did see that with you when you were young, like you respected life around you, and that's perhaps got to do with the fact that we didn't demand you do all this ritual good or not good, which every society demands to some degree. You could feel that naturally, that there'd be no reason to be angsty or against or to do "bad" … so that's got to do with trusting too. You trust the child to understand how to behave in society and to discern what in this society is silly, but that this other thing is a practical response to living together…

We're not born isolated. We're born as social beings but we're not trusted to be. That's it.

Four Qs + a Poem with Cindy White and kitty sipple

(with tech and community support by Dawn White)

Sometimes people come into your life and they just speak the same language as you.[1] When your own personal language is grounded in extreme, other-worldly states, the world just sometimes does not get you. Being in a state of madness while living in a sane world is some people's greatest fear, and yet—for some of us—it is just our everyday state of being.

Showing up as an out Mad adult who experiences extreme states is import-ant in the context of youth liberatory movements that actively dismantle sanism.[2] I was a youth who experienced madness, and we want to create a future that allows youth to thrive outside the sanist restraints. I am deeply grateful for my friendship with Cindy, as it allows us to be fully in connecting the insight of youth with the wisdom of adulthood. The only measurement is time, which acts as the currency of extreme states while also being the lan-guage of madness.

This conversation with Cindy is timeless and time-bound but only if it is defined in non-linear time. Each section is sparked by a particular question

---

1   Dawn White helped facilitate both technical and community support for the container of this conversation between Cindy and kitty. Dawn is Cindy's mother and a friend of kitty's.

2   Here is our definition of Sanism: there is a system of oppression, that is foundation-ally built upon adhering to this idea of consensus reality, that is predicated on moral-ity, rationality, logic, intelligence, all of these systems that really are immeasurable, and are completely influenced and defined and controlled by other dominant systems of oppression. To find out more about Sanism, visit *Grounded Futures* podcast where we are a guest on the show https://groundedfutures.com/shows/grounded-futures-show/grounded-futures-show-episode-13-kitty-sipple.

that relates to a theme, which is open to interpretation, closing with Cindy's poetry submission to this anthology. The themes can be siloed but are best connected through curiosity.

Love across all timelines,

kitty

◆

(Maybe youth autonomy and Mad liberation can intersect and it begins when Cindy shows kitty a drawing.)

Q1

kitty: Okay so is that a clown?

Cindy: Yes. I like clowns. Sometimes I see them and sometimes I see them in my dreams.

kitty: I see things in my dreams too. I don't see clowns though. I see other places that are there. Like I can see them in my dreams and they are the actual places. So I can talk to people, as long as they are dreaming as well. So it is not necessarily what I see in my dreams but how I dream. I also have a lot of control in my dreams. Like I can make things happen in my dreams.

Cindy: Lucid dreaming?

kitty: Yeah. Do you know, do you lucid dream?

Cindy: Mm-hmm.

kitty: Yeah it is kind of neat, I mean it is kind of neat. Sometimes it is hard. When did you start lucid dreaming?

Cindy: About five years old.

kitty: Yeah, same. I think I was pretty young, like three, because then I learned I could do things in my dreams.

Cindy: I am pretty sure I was way younger though because I used to have night terrors.

kitty: Same, same, yup. I think those came before I realized that I could lucid dream. Is that what happened to you?

Dawn: Actually you had night terrors when you first came to us. You were three and a half.

Cindy: I was about to say three.

kitty: Yup, that's right. About the same time as me.

Q2

kitty: Do you remember the first time we met?

Cindy: Yeah.

kitty: How long ago was that?

Cindy: Two years.

kitty: Wow it seems like much longer, wow. I was so excited to meet you for the first time. Do you remember what we talked about?

Cindy: I think it was about dreams and schizophrenia.

kitty: Yup, I told you about hearing voices and we talked about hearing music. I still hear music. I heard drums the other day. Do you still hear music?

Cindy: Yeah.

kitty: Do you ever… Do you ever put it together with the words you write?

Cindy: Yeah.

kitty: Oh, that's cool. I would definitely listen to music that you make.

(break in conversation because of a dissociative moment)

Q3

kitty: Is there anything that you wanted to share with me?

Cindy: Yes, but I don't know how to put it out.

Dawn: However you want.

Cindy: They/them thing.

kitty: Are you asking about my pronouns?

Cindy: Yes.

kitty: So I use they/them pronouns and I started using them about four years ago. I am neither a man nor a woman. I am trans non binary so that they/them pronouns feel non gendered. I also use *them* because of multiplicity—being multiple—because "they" can be singular and "they" can also be plural. Have you been thinking about they/them pronouns?

Cindy: I am not sure. To me I never felt like I was a girl or a boy. I don't want to make people have a difficult time saying they/them so I am not really sure what to do.

kitty: That is a very real situation. If you want to change your pronouns, that's your right. That is you wanting to show up and be seen in the world as how you feel. If other people have issues with it, that's their problem. It can be hard, especially letting people know that you've changed your pronouns. It is good to have allies around you that do use your pronouns. So you can practice and learn how to go out into the world and maybe ruffle some feathers. I am a feather ruffler.

(laughter)

kitty: Do you also know that sometimes you can use two sets of pronouns?

Cindy: (excited) NO?!

kitty: So you can use she/her AND they/them.

Q4

Cindy: What is dissociation to you?

kitty: So you know how in lucid dreaming you have your physical body that is asleep? Then you have your energetic body, and your energetic body can separate? That action is the same action as disassociation, just not in a stressful situation. Sometimes it is a really big separation and when we come back together, we have this experience similar to what happened earlier. Where it feels like you kind of went somewhere and then came back. It used to be a lot more scary and disorienting. Now it's just something that is part of life. It's an experience and it doesn't always have to be distressing. When it is more intense than usual, that is usually an indicator of a big stress that I am under. So dissociation is an experience but it can also be a flag to something else that is going on. How do you feel about dissociation?

Cindy: Well, I do it a lot on the bus. Like I will be sitting here and then I am like, wait, did I sit on the bus for three times or did I... Like I get confused if I did something or not. And I am also like that in the store, where I am walking, like I will just be walking and I am like why did I come here?

kitty: That happens to me all the time all the time. Do you remember?

Cindy: Sometimes I don't remember.

kitty: Yeah, same.

Cindy: It is like a bit foggy.

kitty: I try to not feel bad about the fog because I am not trying to make my brain foggy. I just try not to feel bad when it happens because it happens, you know, like you said, walking into the store and I don't remember why I walked in here. Also, I think some doors are portals to a different time. You walk in, you forget, you walk back out, you remember. Does that ever happen to you?

Cindy: Yeah.

kitty: This is why I like to say that I am a time traveler. I had a question for you and now I forget.

Cindy: Story of my life.

kitty: Oh gosh, that is like my theme song.

(laughter)

A poem by Cindy White

Just you and me
dancing in a daydream
hoping to find something to take us away.
You're always running
light the world on fire
Home sweet home are lost and gone
Filled with ashes and bones
The world is filled with mean beings that confuse and scare
No one seems to hear you until you are loud.

On Being a Trusted Adult

A conversation between Chris Mercogliano and
Lily Mercogliano Easton

Lately I (Lily) have been thinking a lot about how important an emphasis on kids trusting adults is and how much there is a concept for some adult archetypes like a "Passive Parent" or "Authoritarian Teacher," but not the same conversation around what it is to be a "Trusted Adult." It can be one thing to set an intention to trust kids, but it is easy to immediatelty hit the roadblock of kids not being interested in that adult relationship because they do not trust the person trying to build it.

My father, Chris Mercogliano, has always been a trust mentor for me. Children, from a very young age (elementary-school aged) up until they went to high school, trusted him often at first sight at the Albany Free School, where he taught and later became the school director. When I started working with kids, and particularly when I was working at and leading Brooklyn Free School, I had a similar experience of being, from the start, a trusted adult in that space.

In most settings where we work, my father and I have both been asked how to teach that kind of trust building to other adults. It will hopefully not surprise the reader that this is not something we know how to teach. Our goal in this conversation is to explore how we approach trust in our relationship, and as parents and educators.

Lily: Where did you start on your journey to being trusted by kids?

Chris: In my own childhood, I was given a lot of trust from my mom and allowed into adult space in my family setting in ways that led me to value how important that borderless dynamic is to kids. Then later, I chose places to work where I could be myself, and kids could be themselves.

Lily: I was also one of those kids who found a lot of comfort on the periphery of adult spaces—I have never thought about that before. I started getting paid to be with kids, as a mother's helper, when I was eight and stayed in mostly youth centered work through high school and college, and have continued there in my career as a teacher and director of youth nonprofits. There is an urgency for me to learn when I am working with young people and that dynamic keeps me present.

Chris: There is no question that you cannot teach someone how to make kids trust them. You can teach people how to be better listeners, especially if that work starts as young adults, but no, you cannot teach someone to be relaxed and real with kids in the way they need. That has to come from a person doing their own personal growth and unconsciously being at ease with kids.

Lily: What ways can adults communicate to kids that they believe them and can be trusted?

Chris: Even when my own kids were young I knew that, in a relative way, they knew as much as I did. Sure, I was the parent and they were the children, but as eight-year-old's they knew so much about their needs and the needs around them. They had strong, clear voices. And I always found that to be true about all ages and types of kids. I am never afraid of angry or edgy kids—and they can sense that. I genuinely accept every child in their totality.

Lily: When I enter a space, I take a moment to notice how a kid is seeing me and to try to discern what it is they are seeking. My goal is to see myself through the eyes of the child, or the group of children. Sometimes it is really important to take up space and be active as the adult in the room. Other times, kids want to know that they can fill that with what they are doing, and in order to trust the adult, they have to see the adult hold back. Judging the difference in needs has to come from an assumption that kids are wonderful and also with the humility to know that what an adult can offer will depend on the individual needs of the young people and that unique situation.

Chris: A lot of people are afraid of children, and kids pick up on that right away. Their inability to trust kids is part of it, but there is an elemental component to how they feel around children that is even more foundational. Most adults are guarded around children. Children's incredible liveliness and aliveness, at an unconscious level, is threatening to a guarded person who has been cut off from their own aliveness. This fear is heightened when the adult is in a position of authority, like a parent or teacher, and even more intense when facing external expectations in regards to how the children in their care should perform. Even after decades of knowing better and striving for something different: the world does not trust children. Still. There is no question that we are not there.

Lily: At the same time, there is so much generational change within our own family. If I look back to my great grandparents versus how my children are growing up in this family... the transformation is incredible. My kids are freer than I was. And I was freer than my parents were.

Starting with each great-grandmother, I can trace women who tried to do something remarkably different in their families. Being intentional about parenting from a place of trust, and being a parent that can be trusted by their kids, comes incrementally and with a lot of continued struggle.

What do kids need most from adults?

Chris: The more I learned about the importance of seeing children's brilliance, the more I wanted to learn. The anthropologist and author Jean Liedloff, who wrote *The Continuum Concept*—the book that coined the term "Attachment Parenting"—said, children need two things and they certainly do not need to be managed. She said that the worst thing you can do to a child is do for them something they can do for themselves. Instead, what they need is to feel worthy and welcome. Period. They do not need anything else. Starting from that baseline, if you truly accept a child, then you will love them unconditionally. If you really listen to kids, and don't talk over them, and don't immediately provide the answers and so on, if you are not managing them, that communicates to kids that you believe in them.

Lily: There is a realness that has to be present in a relationship where kids will feel believed. I have had multiple students as teenagers tell me that they wish their fathers had hit them. And what I understood from what they were really saying is that they wanted authentic communication from their parents. Too much of the communication and parenting they were getting was passive. It was not that they wanted to be abused—they wanted direct and honest feedback and interactions. Saying things nicely is not a substitute for being real with youth and believing in the worth of an authentic relationship.

Kids also need to see that adults care what they think. Being a kid's favorite person on earth is not my priority at all times, but making sure they have solid space and communicating that I care in a very present and deep way… that is enormously important to me.

Chris: Yes, and I really like kids! I just think they are so interesting and amazing. That feeling grows the older I get because kids continue to bring me back to these parts of myself that are more alive.

Lily: How can adults improve their ability to interact with kids from a place of trust instead of fear?

Chris: There is no question that the world is increasingly a fearful place. The answer to not responding to kids from that place of fear is community. Building community requires being truly connected to other people—and not just your own immediate family. When community is present, it really is okay to be vulnerable with each other. And disagreement happens, and is going to happen because people are different.

Young parents on the nuclear-family track have to realize that they need more connection and seek it out. This can start even before a child is born through shared community with other pregnant families who are invested in having a birth framed by trust, or schooling that is influenced by trust.

There is also the opportunity to build community with older people—either within a biological family or within a chosen family. As an adult, I got to a place of having a solid peer relationship with my own mom. Now that my kids are grown, and have their own kids, we have this powerful peer to peer connection and it is so cool. My kids are definitely better parents than I was. In so many ways, my wife and I were not such great parents. But we planted seeds.

Lily: I get humbled when I remember that having radical politics, or a radical education style, is not a substitute for how we have to trust our kids at home and be as parents. Or how we have to show up for youth in our neighborhoods, workplaces, and in a global sense.

◆

A lot of times my parents did respond to me from a place of fear, especially when I was very young. What made a huge difference over time was how much they continued to evolve, listen to me, and believe in the way I saw the world. And also how much they connected me to many adults who I could trust.

As an adult now, I still feel as if I am a child with my dad, in the sense that I do not consider him a peer. But our relationship has shifted now that we are both adults. Parenting and living close to my parents has been a lot about forgiveness—forgiving my parents for big mistakes they made when I was a kid now that we are all adults and getting to forge a new relationship in the context of my own kids, and also forgiveness of myself for still needing to learn so much as a parent and an adult. I cannot imagine there will ever be a time in my life when I am not challenging what I believe, or my own behavior as a result of reflecting on what youth need.

Solidarity Begins at Home, or A Landing Pad Without Borders

By carla joy bergman

"As we give you roots, you give us wings."—Richard Van Camp, *We Sang You Home*
"A man's maturity consists in having found again the seriousness one had as a child, at play."
—Nietzsche, *Beyond Good and Evil*

If you subscribe to the notion that relationships compose the world, and being in these relationships brings us freedom, then it ought to follow that the relationships we are in must be deeply respectful and mutually beneficial to all involved. Since I was a young adult, I have been interested in how we aim for this in our relationships with young people, whether as parents, adult friends, or community members. In particular, I like to spend time talking about our day-to-day relationships with young folks in our homes, in our collectives, in our movements, and in our communities. Anywhere that we share space with kids.

Animating my home and community-organizing worlds were (and are) the ideas and the actions of solidarity and autonomy. I feel that, for a thriving now and a thriving future, we must be organizing and creating connections based in mutual aid, experimentation, care, and generosity, but it must also be intergenerational. I continue to find inspiration in the autonomous zones and prefigurative projects from around the world, where all members of the community are included in genuine ways. And this inspiration grows as we see a groundswell of Indigenous resurgence movements around the world—all of which provide examples of creating alternatives to the dominant order, engendering concrete examples and lifeways of re-imagining autonomous, thriving, and a decolonial future for all members in the community.

These interwoven organizing ideas took some time to take hold in my life. So, first I want to share a bit about how my family connected to threads of solidarity, where our home life began to be woven into our communities in powerful ways, blurring the borders between private and public.

As a parent, alongside my partner, over the years, we aimed to have an autonomous and thriving home. What that means is we strive to have a relationship-centered home that is consensual and respectful, and at the root is a profound trust that our kids know more about what they need and want than we could ever know. I won't go into too much detail of our home life, but I will write briefly about school because it's part of how we got to creating these webs of connections.

When my eldest, Zach, was a baby, we grappled with how we were going to deal with school. We asked ourselves: how is forcing a kid to go to a space five days a week, autonomously driven? We were working-class parents, and I was in university at the time and couldn't even imagine any other way… By the time Zach was in grade 2, we saw his lights go out, the passion around learning that he always had, began to diminish. So we intervened. We made some big changes: I quit school, we got roommates, and we entered into a world of unschooling/deschooling. In other words, we trusted each other, and our kid entered into a world of life learning that was rooted in community and solidarity. From there, we all engaged in co-learning with a passionate unschooling ethos, where we followed our curiosity and interests. We were tremendously lucky to be part of a large unschooling and democratic-schooling community. We co-learned with so many other families and rad momma mentors, and learned alongside many other kids—it was incredible! I found so much thriving in these connections. Over time, what was hard was a disconnect between my politics as an organizer and as a parent. Because to me, what I was seeing was how most kids and families couldn't opt out of school.

Back to solidarity. I started asking the question how we could create spaces where any kid could have access to a deschooling, youth liberated environment, where we could actively push against the social borders of ageism. It didn't take too long to find a solution because we were able to find a space like this in our neighborhood, called the Purple Thistle Centre.[1] The Thistle was a youth-run arts and activism Centre that ran for fifteen years in Vancouver on the occupied lands of the xwməθkwəy̓əm (Musqueam), Skwxwú7mesh (Squamish), and səlílwətaʔɬ/Selilwitulh (Tsleil-Waututh) people. The project was founded in 2001 by one adult, Matt Hern, and six youth, who together created ways for youth to run a space and co-learn and thrive together. The Thistle was intentionally created to think about this issue of solidarity with kids who have to go to school, and so it was open after school hours and weekends,

---

1   Https://purplethistle.ca. Alongside Corin Browne, I made a short documentary about the project: https://vimeo.com/208059591.

and free to use. With a penchant for making art, Zach ended up plugging into the Thistle by age eleven. I soon followed, and together we were part of the project for seven years. Together, we co-created, with a large community of young folks, and many older folks too, a thriving autonomous space where learning together went beyond the physical building, and being in solidarity with many other movements and struggles were both at the heart of all we did.

Still learning

If Zach taught me about how to truly trust a young person, my youngest son, Liam, has taught me about power. I used to organize with youth in my home and in community, thinking about empowerment—how can we empower youth more?—and I wasn't alone; the materials out of most radical and less radical spaces talk about empowering others. This is what my nine-year-old said to me at the time, in response to that rhetoric: "I don't need to be empowered by adults; I need them to stop having power over me." This statement fundamentally changed how I organized from that moment on. When we have more power in these situations, it's not about sharing it or empowering others, it's about getting out of the way of their power and truly trusting them to use it. I am constantly amazed, although never surprised, how much learning there is to gain from the youngest members of our communities. So with this nuanced relationship to our personal powers, we constantly worked on ways to thrive individually and together, but, in some ways it still felt cut off from the many folks in the neighborhood.

While the Thistle was this incredible public project that worked to undo ageism and support youth liberation, I started to think more about home and the private life of kids and their oppression there. Adult supremacy is a barrier to transformation and to children's thriving in all parts of society. Oppression and violence against children in the home—in particular spanking—is reportedly high in the US alone, and according to Dr. Toby Rollo, "There was a committee report in the US that estimated unreported child mortality at the hands of parents and caretakers to be very high."[2] Many of the adults at the Thistle had informally set up our homes as an extension, in a variety of ways, to the Thistle (many of the youth had keys to my home and were invited to share space with us often) attempting to blur the lines between private and public.

---

2   Toby Rollo, "Feral Children: Settler Colonialism, Progress, and the Figure of the Child," *Settler Colonial Studies* 8 (2018): 60–79.

And we also did this because many kids didn't have great homes to go to after Thistle hours.

It's around this time that I started using the phrase *solidarity begins at home* as a way to highlight the separation that is often reinforced by radical communities. On the one hand, we want to upend the hetero-normative-nuclear-patriarchy home, but on the other hand, there's still this impulse to cut home life off from the movements. I am grateful for the decades of vital work being done to denuclearize the family and the home, and we can especially look for inspiration to many LGBTQ+ folks' ways of building homes and kin that fall outside of these patriarchal and oppressive structures. However, it's important to note that the oppression of kids isn't only a nuclear family problem.

The struggle, to me, is how do we have these little pockets of solidarity and autonomy while the majority of our communities are living amid the systems that keep them cut off from this kind of collective thriving and from being involved in other forms of life that include children in sincere ways? How do we break down the borders between adult and kid? Of course, the other, often more desired option by activists and organizers is to fight for large-scale change, so that if we have a massive overhaul revolution, all will change. But I am not convinced that's going to fix this issue of ageism against young folks, or many of our social inequalities that continue to harm our community members.

To me, it's no wonder that most large autonomous movements are not that long lasting. Because when so many members of our communities are left out of planning and organizing ... where so many are socially silenced, how can it take hold over time? Of course, there are other forces crushing these movements, but this is also a problem. And many of these outliers, folks who are left out, are not just kids, they often include women, disabled, BIPOC, LGBTQ+ folks, and other folks who are not part of a social bias of what it means or looks like to have the social power or knowledge to provide ideas on how to enact change.

These often-normalized social fractures in our communities are deadly real and work to chip away at our relationships, causing rifts in our social bonds with each other. This makes it challenging for movements to take root. Or to put it another way: The roots are often still there, deep in the ground, but there's a disconnect, or more precisely there are institutions built on top of the buried social ways of being in relationship that cut us off from our more autonomous and communal ways of being together. And children spend a great deal of their lives locked away in one of these institutions.

I don't want to be misunderstood here. I'm not suggesting that we need to teach autonomy to kids, or create more institutions. That would only reinforce the disconnect, and be an utter disaster. What we need to do is rethink, or evoke other ways of being in relationship with kids. Which means including them consensually in the conversations on how to create these new ways of being together.

Time weaving

It's true that when the conditions are such, like they were at the Thistle, autonomy can emerge, ethically, in relationship and in specific context. But it has to be decided upon and created by and with the folks who are in the room. The hegemonic forms of life, the colonial ideology (white-heteronormative-patriarchal—from here on I'll just say Empire) that has been at work for centuries creating infrastructure and institutions to cut us off from our roots, and ultimately from our relationships with each other and the more-than-human kin is what we need to dismantle while we reclaim our own decolonial forms of life. We can locate some of this by looking to the past at how the borders between folks were set up by design. We can trace how Empire removed responsibility for each other from most of our social situations; institutions and industrial production have taken away our capacity to be responsible for raising kids, educating ourselves, growing our food, building our dwellings, and so on. The state removal and displacement of many of our social relationships is ongoing, and it is done primarily through these institutions.

At the edges, there is hope. It comes down to place, where we live, our home, our ecologies, the land. All over the world there are many Indigenous lifeways and knowledges that were not fully colonized, and we are seeing small and massive resurgences. From Ireland, to the Sámi in Norway, to the Ainu in Japan, to the Māori, and of course to South and North America where thousands of Indigenous nations continue to rise up and demand their rights to their land, and reclaim their languages and lifeways. It's awe-inspiring. These fierce and loving decolonial and autonomous communities that are often low to the ground, but sometimes larger (like the Zapatista and Rojava communities), are the largest cracks in Empire. They provide some pathways and inspiration to all of us wanting a better world. These movements and autonomous outbursts are constantly rising, emerging, although not necessarily in automatic autonomous ways, because they've been slowly building over time, or were never fully lost. As the Indigenous scholar Glen Coulthard said to us in an interview we did for *Joyful Militancy*: "Emergent doesn't mean entirely new, because those relationships to place are not new. They've always been there, and are always re-emerging. It comes in cycles."[3]

These acts of cultural reclamation, which is both the recovery of a people's languages and cultural practices, is on the rise. There is a deep connection to place, reconnecting with kin across age and abilities, and with the more-than-humans, creating the conditions for reciprocal and decolonial relationships with each other and the land. In some—and in probably more than I know—kids are part of the resurgence, especially with regards to language learning. Children are seen as integral members of their communities, especially because most Indigenous cultures think beyond the one current generation. But not all. Children are often still marginalized and cut off from the day-to-day life of adults. They are often sent to school all day long, where they are "protected." Capitalism forces us to make decisions that are in direct conflict with our values, but some still believe that children are to be educated away from community. This seems to be the one colonial strong hold in many of the autonomous and Indigenous movements around the world. And I think it's part of the story of why many of these movements stagnate, or are easily squashed.

Some will argue that kids have always been protected, kept outside of the adult world, or isolated in nuclear families, away from community. But these social borders were built. It was part of the colonial plan, and it was part of industrial capitalism's plan. The plan is to prepare kids to be workers, and to assimilate them away from their customs and lifeways, through state-led education and schooling. Colonizers know that to assimilate the children is the best way to change a culture in one generation. Despite this stronghold, there have always been other ways of being and relating to kids that strengthens our bonds with each other. And resistance was always happening alongside the State's control tactics.

Entangled thriving:
A case for including kids in sincere ways

Many Indigenous scholars have written that, before colonization, there were no clear social divides between the genders and ages in their communities.[4]

---

3   Interview with Glen Coulthard, by Nick Montgomery and carla bergman. Email, November 2, 2015.

4   See Leanne Betasamosake Simpson writings, as well as many others.

And, bell hooks points to traditions of informal adoption in Black communities, in which people adopted and cared for children in ways that were communally recognized but never sanctioned by the State.[5] In the book *Escaping Education*, Madhu Suri Prakash and Gustavo Esteva trace how, in many places in India and Mexico, by the time children were five years old, they were expected to be full members of their communities. There are many more stories like this from all around the world that help us see what has been lost, and maybe how we can reclaim some of it today.

But, we need to dig deep, and recover these roots, these forms of lives, not only to have a more equitable and just world for all humans, but to save the planet and the more-than-humans. Making kin (that stretches across species and includes the land), according to Donna Haraway, "is perhaps the hardest and most urgent part" of our survival. We also need to reimagine how we make kin with kids. Part of this work comes from displacing settler colonialism and decentering the nuclear family, both of which are destroying kids' autonomy and participation in community. But how do we start? We need to think about how we co-create with kids. What would it be like? When we interviewed Leanne Betasamosake Simpson about children and self-determination she said:

> How change happens matters to me, which is why I don't spend much time lobbying the state. I believe in creating the change on the ground, and creating and living the alternatives. In my nation, children and Elders are critical, and it means we organize differently. You can't invite kids to a boring twelve-hour meeting and then get frustrated because they are bored or frustrated because they won't stay with the child care worker they've never met.... I think we actually need to do less organizing and more movement building. Right now, we have activists, not leaders. We have actions, not community. My kids are also fundamentally not interested in "the movement." They are, however, fundamentally interested in doing things.[6]

What Leanne points to is important. We can't just invite kids into our structures and ways we do things, we have to start over. As well, and this is just good for us all, we need to find more ways to come together in ceremony and

---

5   bell hooks, *Outlaw Culture: Resisting Representations* (New York: Routledge, 2006), 249.

6   Interview with Leanne Betasamosake Simpson, by Nick Montgomery and carla bergman, November 2, 2015.

celebration that is not culturally appropriating, because to me it is one of the best ways to sow the seeds of trust and friendship across age and difference. It is also a way to counter the stronghold of liberalism and individualism, as ceremony and celebration are situated in community. Everyone we interviewed for *Joyful Militancy* who experienced situations of longer term and meaningful autonomy and self-determination said there were always built-in gatherings that were celebratory, joyful. The Zapatistas are very vocal about this.

I think it's important for us to draw on past examples of resistance to inspire us, and this often requires us to look hard for them because the dominant narratives are often patriarchal and colonial, and deeply ageist. Hearing more stories that provide another way of surviving and thriving can be essential to our current survival. To work to unearth these knowledges, to look back to the stories, but also tuning in to the relationships we are in today is the balance we must strive for—and it must include uncovering the lost stories of how we were in community with children.

While I take massive inspiration from the movements for autonomy and revolution today, I wonder where are the kids? Are they in school? Where are they? And, alongside that I ask: how do we imagine a way to cultivate autonomy and self-determination in our cities, while capitalism tears apart our lives, continues to displace many of us? And how can we do this across cultural and age divides, particularly with children? One thing I have seen over and over again, in my research on social movements that include kids, is that you must create ways to come together to learn, ways that are rooted in autonomy and are pedagogically decolonial.

"Trust is always a gift and a risk."

Projects like the Thistle and Universidad de la Tierra in Oaxaca, Mexico,[7] were terrific at holding onto this de-institutional ethics while also supporting the needs of the community to survive and thrive under conflicting systems (e.g. gain skills that will ensure they can make a living). Deschooling, or unschooling, or alternatives to schooling are pathways to co-create learning spaces for all ages, to connect folks, build stronger communities, and enact change. They are the common grounds for cutting across this age divide, and through them, it can happen immediately. These spaces and projects often work as sites to increase

---

7   Universidad de la Tierra is an alternative to university and community run space located in Oaxaca, Mexico: https://unitierraoax.org

our personal and collective power to act and respond to the violence and oppression affecting many, a way to respond in solidarity to our communities in need. These alternatives to school and social spaces are concrete ways to break free of the rigid social roles that divide adults and kids, and help us build larger webs of communities that include many ages and abilities.

Most of my work to date has been about creating alternatives to schooling with my community, so I have a bit to share on how to do this across age. And it's pretty basic: get together with a group of friends (hopefully you or they know some kids!) and ask each other questions about how you want to learn together. What do you want to learn together? With a guiding question like: How do we co-create a space that provides skill sharing, accessible and rigorous ways of learning and creating together (that is hopefully free, or at least financially accessible), that is rooted in dignity and self-determination, and creates a thriving life for all?[8]

Self-determination movements for learning must be rooted in autonomy and co-learning. Co-learning is about centering relationships first, and that is a solid starting point for achieving collective thriving, while it also causes cracks in Empire and sustained radical change. It's also an invitation into counteracting ageism, because a youth can teach an adult, be responsible for the space, for each other, and themselves. This co-learning, skill sharing, and mentoring goes in all directions, and we can start to undo ageism in these smaller acts. In doing so, the rigid, but socially constructed borders would begin to come down. Imagine a world where every relationship we had was reciprocal and consent-based instead of extractive, where trust and responsibility were the foundation. What kind of community would we have?

Solidarity takes root in listening

"Children don't get traumatized because of the hurt, they get traumatized because they are alone with the hurt."
—Gabor Maté, *The Wisdom of Trauma*

Trust in ourselves and trust in each other is key, and in order to trust we need

---

8   This really works. I used it a lot in different scenarios over the past two decades and I deepened how to do this well from working with Matt Hern, as it was how the Thistle began.

to listen more. Trust and listening go together and are the foundation of our survival. Of course, whose ideas are adopted and how folks decide to enact them is deeply complex and not an easy road; lots of questions are needed, and even more listening. It's a messy process and at times it will be a slow one, because justice isn't an immediate fix. As Toby Rollo reminds us: "Social justice is an intergenerational project. The hardest thing to accept is that you're not going to be the one who crosses the finish line. It's not a sprint. It's not a marathon. It's a relay."[9]

To me, autonomy functions best in smaller communities where we can truly ask the necessary questions together, work across differences, make mistakes, and where a deep trust can be nurtured and felt. We must hang onto uncertainty, similar to the Zapatistas' notion *preguntando caminamos*: "asking, we walk." Autonomy is a fierce commitment to emergent forms of life in the cracks of Empire, and the values, responsibilities, and questions that sustain them, especially with our youngest. But we also must be committed to building webs of solidarities that stretch beyond our autonomy projects, to ensure thriving and justice for all.

These brave acts of love and care that stretch across differences—especially with children—these acts that undo Empire's fierce hold on our everyday existence, are often pushed to the margins as incongruitous, but we know better. As Homero Aridjis said: "The music of the night is not in the stars but in the darkness between them."[10] In other words: autonomy is already happening, we just can't see it all. So, I give my deepest gratitude to the many that are already working on dismantling Empire's hold on our lives and our relationships, especially with kids. Thank you to all these unheard or less-heard stories that find their way to us in a whisper on the winds of change. We are listening.

---

9   Toby Rollo in conversation with the author in October 2019.

10   Homero Aridjis, "Romantic," in *Eyes to See Otherwise: Selected Poems* (New York: New Directions, 2002), 1–3. References are to line.

Listen... Adults!

By Curiousism Cyphers

> "There is a voice that doesn't use words. Listen."
> —Jalal ad-Din Rumi

colonizers violently scratched lines across territories of love

fungi ancestors wrapped their tendrils around their human kin, whispering memories into their heart's DNA

poisonous borderlines settling in, leaving traces on the body, scars that imprint fear

that are like an odorless gas mutating across generations choking our potential

Babies gassy coughs rejecting the fear, adults learning this new love language

Inflamed eyes squint through campfires kindled with poison oak

We held hands and planted seeds on the ruins, sprouts came and cleansed the poison smoke

Following the coughs to the wild edges, where roses peek, the fog welcoming the dew drops that signal the rain

Dropping onto our senses' power as the fog-like-gas begins to evaporate

Lineages of lovelines feel their way across the cellular maps, our babies cough's fade

Beyond the edges Holt is casting with the stars "Babies are nice people" laughing he passes the wand on to you

A wand that's been passed and is being passed through layers of time

We don't need scientific papers or "facts" to know spanking is violence

And each spank echoes for seven generations, pain that ripples verbalized through silence

We are far from the first, this is how we heal

Being marked truant on attendance sheets let's become absent to institutions that desocialize

Fear is the enemy of learning, we gaze through the trickster's logic of coercion
Compete in class and receive a recess where even the binaries materialize as
    seesaws
With persuasion on one end and punishment on the other
The greatest betrayal? They tried to teach the land wasn't a teacher, wasn't a
    relative, wasn't love but something to be harnessed and controlled
Ancestors glide through walls and duck and cover drills and lead us away
Hugging us in the sunlight while fungi thrives and pushes through the clay
Children are born learners, they know when they are being trusted and when
    they are not
They know there's little difference between barbwire and walled gardens
Children are creators, producers, energy, treasures, necessary to health and
    survival
Abandoning the metal detectors and board budgets we reach for so much
    more even if it's a summitless summit
Children love the land that is why they learn so well from it

Childing the World

By Toby Rollo

Centering childhood

My aim in the following is to stage a series of interventions into contemporary activism and emancipatory scholarship. I would like to draw attention to the idea that peace and justice are essentially intergenerational projects that require the centering of children at a fundamental level. This process of centering the child in liberatory theory and practice I will refer to as *childing*. I begin by arguing that we must change how we view childhood itself. I then discuss the manifold ways in which oppression of the young structures the institutions of domination that activists concerned with peace, justice, and the environment wish to dismantle.

Virtually every young person in the world has experienced discrimination, exclusion, coercion, and violence for no other reason than that they are a child. Intersectional approaches have cautioned us against crude reductionism, showing how race, class, gender, and ability overlap and converge in distinct ways to produce diverse experiences of domination. In addition to the better understood intersections of one's experience and identity, childhood on its own is foundational. Even those who occupy the most privileged subject positions in society have experienced it. It is in childhood that we are taught to be ashamed of ourselves for being small, weak, uncoordinated, ignorant, and dependent on adults. It is in childhood that we are taught that we must strive to overcome these deficits if we are to become fully human. It is in childhood that we are taught that those who are big, strong, competent, knowledgeable, and autonomous must use coercion to shepherd the child out of their debased animal condition. It is in childhood that we are taught that resistance to discipline is both futile and immoral. It is in childhood that we are taught how any failure to attain the sacred markers of maturity reflect a defect in our nature or character. The child experiences oppression precisely because they are a child, and this debasement and dehumanization produces trauma that robs human beings of their self-worth and empathy for others, conditioning individuals to see domination and exploitation as normal, natural, and necessary.

Childhood is, therefore, the originary site—ground zero—of all systems of domination, the position where all forms of oppression are produced and reproduced. As psychiatrist Dr. Chester Pierce, who coined the terms "microaggression" and "childism," observed, discrimination against children "is the basic form of oppression in our society and underlies all alienation and violence, for it teaches everyone how to be an oppressor and makes them focus on the exercise of raw power rather than on volitional humaneness."[1] The trauma of childhood is the organizing structure of our dehumanizing discourses of race, class, gender, and ability. All forms of domination are prefigured, in both form and content, by the domination of the child.

Accordingly, to treat the child as a full human being is to cut at the very roots of oppression—a radical and revolutionary first step in any struggle for freedom based on care and interdependence rather than on violence and hierarchy. To the degree that we ignore children and childhood, we ensure that our progressive victories will be temporary, that our political and social gains will swiftly erode, and we might even unintentionally reinscribe more pernicious forms of tyranny.

From birth, the young present to those around them an ethical demand for care and interdependence. Alongside this primordial relational demand, children exercise creative resistance to individuals and systems that deny care and neglect interdependence. Thus, the child is always already *childing* the world in practice. Adults are capable of childing practices, as well, insofar as we can embody the creative, curious, spontaneous, and non-representational form of agency and cognition that disrupts norms, and which we prioritized in our youth. Childing can also take the form of disruptive intellectual critique directed at systems of thought, ideologies, and worldviews. Just as *queering* and *cripping* critiques reveal hidden dynamics of power rooted in heteronormativity and ableism, *childing* centers the child in ways that reveal where and how oppression of the young configures our relationships, institutions, and cultures.

---

1   Chester M. Pierce and Gail B. Allen, "Childism," *Psychiatric Annals* 5 (1975): 266–70.

Rethinking childhood?

Childing as critique necessarily begins with a radical shift in how we understand childhood itself. Childhood is not a temporary or provisional stage or phase in a developmental process. The child is not in a state of becoming more human and less animal. A child is not a developing, defective, deficient, or less-than-fully-human being. Rather, the childhood is a modality of being in which certain forms of human agency—the child's unmediated, exploratory, and experimental ways of engaging with the world—are most prominent and privileged. Childhood is merely a different *way* of being, one that is not exclusive to youth. Childhood capacities are never lost, abandoned, or displaced but, rather, carried throughout our lives.

Adulthood does not mark the apex in some trajectory of development away from the world and toward something greater. What many of us become as we grow older is a being who can live both a mediated and an unmediated life, as one who can entertain intellectual and representational propositions *about* the world while also experiencing, navigating, and exploring the world with an immediacy that defies representation. To the extent that we know *how* to do something like ride a bike, we are children. To the extent that we know *that* a bike is a series of simple materials and mechanisms, we are adults. Throughout most of our lives, to a greater or lesser extent, we are both. But neither modality is inherently superior to the other, nor more vital for supporting ethical and political life.

For most of western history, adults have defined human freedom and "the good life" in explicit opposition to the child. Order and justice became tendentiously associated with adult capacities for virtue in judgment, piety, and faith, or universalizing reason, over and against those who did not possess such quasi-divine faculties. In the West, childhood has been defined in contradistinction to freedom and goodness, and positioned as the source of worldly vice, sin, and irrationality that threatens to turn order into chaos. As I will discuss below, the resulting exclusions of childhood immediacy, care, and interdependence have been catastrophic for human beings and the world we inhabit.

In centering childhood, we are confronted with our primordial orientation of care and attentiveness to others and the world. Our bodies remember our immersion in life, cradled by tree branches or the arms of a loving adult. We are reminded of how we navigated the inextricable interdependences of bodies and the world. As we grow older, many of us learn to form abstract propositions about these modes of being, representing them through signs and symbols to ourselves and others. But even among philosophers, such sophisticated and formal ways of thinking occupy rare moments of everyday life. Most of our time is spent not in theory but in practice—not as adults but as children—moving through our environments, interacting, and caring for others.

Childing historical constructions of the figure of the child involves a fundamental overhaul of basic conceptions of agency, autonomy, and freedom. It demands a phenomenological revision of our conception of the human, away from the sole veneration of speech and reason, allegedly secured by our escape from childhood, toward a vision of humanity characterized by differences and pluralities.

Class, political economy, and the environment

The young represent the originary exploited class. As far back as the historical record goes in the West, the bodies and labor of children were viewed as belonging to adults. Children were the first form of property, and mass child labor was central to every agricultural and industrial revolution—to the production of surplus resources along with the amassing and centralization of wealth. Child labor afforded adults with the resources and leisure time needed to develop the arts, sciences, and philosophy. In short, western civilization was built on the sweat and blood of its children. During the classical era of European history, children were essential to the accumulation of wealth. The larger the family or clan, the more land could be cultivated and defended, and the more wealth could be generated. Wealthy clans grew into chiefdoms, which grew into kingdoms, which amalgamated into empires. Empires secured wealth through child labor. In ancient Rome, those who were too poor to pay taxes and could only offer their children (*proles*) as laborers for the empire were referred to as the *proletarius*. Child labor went on to become the primary engine of agrarian feudalism and advances in technological warfare before propelling the economic shift to industrial capitalism, where once again the proletarians had only their labor and the labor of their children to offer up to the capitalist. Today, the global economy would fall to pieces without the labor of children in "developing" nations, where they provide much of the agricultural, textile, and manufacturing labor, not to mention the mining of minerals required for our modern digital economy.

Childing economic history and political economy provides insight into the puzzle of why European societies developed into modern liberal capitalist states while many Indigenous cultures remained "primitive" and stateless. One major factor is that many (though not all) Indigenous cultures did not view children as exploitable property, and so did not lay the groundwork for a similar series of violent processes involving agricultural revolutions, a massive continuous surplus of resources, the amassing and centralization of wealth, the building of empires, or the leisure time and wealth required to make massive investments in technologies of war and exploitation. Many Indigenous cultures were just not interested in destroying their children or the worlds that their children would inherit. They also viewed species in the natural world as agential, ensouled, and on equal footing with human beings. For many, there simply is no hierarchy of godly man over debased nature, such that the growth of the child represents an ascent out of slavish animal passivity into divine human activity. So, whereas European economic systems "advanced" because they were constructed to serve the immediate desires of the adult, many Indigenous systems remained Indigenous because they made decisions based on the needs of children and generations to come.

Childing the area of political economy reveals how civilization itself is founded, in theory and practice, on the exploitation and destruction of the child for the benefit of adults. In the west, various moral and philosophical schemes were constructed for the purpose of rationalizing and justifying the destruction of children and the natural world to fulfil the desires of adults. Whether it was the expectations of God, or the dictates of universal reason, the conclusion was that man ought to (is obligated to) use reason to exercise dominion over the child and the natural world. The result is a cultural discourse that celebrates the empire of reason as normal, natural, and necessary. The legacy has been one of extinction and perhaps irreversible damage to global climate and ecosystems. Such a legacy can only be addressed by *childing* our economic systems to center the agency of the child. Centering the agency of childhood orients us toward a more Indigenous economics and ecology rooted firmly in care and interdependence. *Childing* the way we sustain ourselves in the world encourages us to pursue immediate, local, and sustainable practices. The world can absorb the footprints of children indefinitely. The *childing* approach, through its deep recognition of care and interdependence, allows us to think about responsibilities to protect youth from coercion, manipulation, harassment, exploitation, and assault. This is especially important because, once rendered as fungible objects that could be bought, sold, and used with impunity, the child is forever at risk of fetishization and abuse.

Sex and gender

The recognition that child labor was integral to the production of greater wealth and leisure time meant that women became valued primarily for their reproductive ability. Children became the center of gravity in a new domain, dominion, and form of domination: the private domestic sphere to which women remain bound to this day, and which remains separate from the public world of politics, philosophy, and art enjoyed by men. The reliable (re)production of children also requires the maintenance of strict gender and sex binaries. Deviance from sex and gender binaries threatens to decouple desire from the reproductive organization of domestic life, and it is for this reason that the child becomes the center of reactionary appeals to the sanctity of the traditional family. Traditionalists are preoccupied with feudal constructions of family wealth, legacy, and reputation, and correctly view traditional moral and political order as founded on the reproductive domestic sphere. Behind this anxiety over experimentation lays an accurate prediction: if left to their own devices, the young would eventually remake the world of sex and gender.

Childing sex and gender begins with a recognition that children come into the world agenderous—without gender identity or expression. Through the creative agency of the child in relations of care, we gradually develop intimacies and desires, some of which may eventually become sexual. These do not belong to any established adult concepts or categories. Many non-western cultures harness this spontaneous formation of desire, which results in ever-evolving practices and performances. Concepts of queer, non-binary, and agender come closest to describing this power to arrive at unique and personal desires and predilections for intimacy unbound by reproductive sex and unconstrained by polarized binaries, fluidities, or spectrums between the artificial poles of masculine and feminine. Insofar as they conform to western notions of masculine and feminine, *homo*sexual and *trans*gender identities and expressions are bound to, and part of, the ecosystem of western *hetero*sexuality and gendering. In the absence of such imposed binary frameworks of desire, youth are free to construct a postgendered society devoid of dysphoria-inducing misalignments of hetero/homo/transnormative embodiments and gender practices.

Race and colonialism

The figure of the child serves as the paradigmatic starting point in western historical, cultural, and biological stories. Without the concept of the child, there is no concept of teleological progress from child to adult, and so no narrative of development from primitive to civilized, and therefore no normative framework upon which to construct an evolutionary narrative about differences between groups of human beings. Consider that non-western peoples were from the outset conceived as the "child races," with their appearance serving as a marker of permanent childhood. Likewise, "white" skin became the marker of civilized adulthood. What it means to be white and civilized is precisely what it means to be an adult and, therefore, to be fully human. To be immature, infantile, underdeveloped, uncivilized, backward, stunted, degenerative, regressive, barbaric, savage, lawless, and criminal is, in the end, precisely what it means to be a child. Just as children have been treated as property, fetishized, and used for labor, the moment Black and Indigenous peoples were classified as "child races" they, too, were immediately positioned to be exploited and fetishized, as well as open to the naturalized violence and punishment required to tame the lawless and irrational child. Any refusal to obey or to concede represents a challenge to the natural order, the original sin of disobedience to authority.

In the wake of the abolition of slavery, when newly freed Black children joined white children on the streets as beggars and orphans, society grew concerned with the future of whiteness. And so began a cultural reconceptualizing of white youth as quasi-adults, "young adults," and proto-citizens who benefit from the legal "presumption of innocence" historically restricted to adults and denied to members of the "child races." Anxiety over the future of whiteness, which is at its core anxiety over future of adult privilege, required that white youth be elevated, at least partially, out of the debased condition of childhood. Black and Indigenous peoples were to remain perpetual children, no matter what their age. *Childing* as critique pulls the rug out from under these racial discourses by denying the distinction between child and adult that structures race. Childing lays bare how the historical, cultural, and evolutionary concepts of race are predicated entirely on an artificial degradation of the child as mere animal and the veneration of the adult as fully human.

Disability

Within the western developmental paradigm, any failure to escape child-hood—that is, to achieve and maintain the complete form and abilities associated with adulthood—is considered a tragic and lamentable failure to become human. Thus, *disability* is defined as an interruption in the "normal" and "natural" fulfillment of the ontogenic *telos* of human development from infant to mature adult. A *childing* lens rejects the notion that adulthood is an achievement and recognizes it simply as a different way of being fully human, which exists alongside other modalities of human agency associated with care and interdependence, which are neither unnecessary nor inferior to adult forms of agency.

To address disability, we must understand that it is structured according to a degraded notion of childhood as a stage closer to animal than human. We see this expressed in the way levels of intellectual or cognitive "disability" are indexed against alleged stages of childhood development. Not only is IQ an age-based metric of intelligence, but the terminology of cognitive disability itself (i.e., fool, moron, idiot, imbecile, etc.) are all defined with reference to the child's progression through various intellectual benchmarks. The "moron" is someone whose cognitive development is that of someone between the ages of ten to twelve years old. The "imbecile" has the mental age of someone four to ten years old. The "idiot" has the mind of someone three years old or younger. Historically, these classifications have corresponded to distinct forms of labor—the labor deemed suitable for children of different ages, as well as adults who cognitively or intellectually remain children, mired in a world of necessity and immediacy rather than freedom and transcendence. And so, IQ and "feeble-mindedness" become a way of designating adults to the labor normally designated to children.

To be intellectually disabled, then, is to be fixed or arrested at an arbitrarily designated stage of childhood development. Likewise, to be physically disabled is to require assistance to move, walk, grasp, or eat in the way we must assist an infant or toddler. In general, disability is shorthand for the dependence of the child and their ethical demand for care, which we already view as a regrettable impingement on the exercise of adult freedom. Without the concept of the adult as a being who defines what it means to be fully human vis-à-vis their abilities to think and act, which is posed in contradistinction to the developing child who is *unable* to function as fully human, there is no basis for the idea of arrested development or *disability*. *Childing* disability entails the elimination of the teleological framework of human development from child to adult, and a recognition of different forms of human as fully human irrespective of age or capacity. This also bears on the participation of differently abled folks in political life.

Intergenerational justice

Like scholarly work, activism is, and only has been, successful to the extent that it centers the child. It begins with an acceptance that childhood is not a stage but a distinct mode of being, and that to be a child is just to privilege a distinct form of agency that is no better or worse than the other forms of agency we come into as we age. This will allow us to dispel notions of natural development, along with its implication of *dis*ability; our racial categories predicated on biological, cultural, or civilizational immaturity; our gender categories constrained by either polarity or fluidity between two parochial and arbitrary ideals: masculine and feminine; and so on.

The slow history of social justice is a record of gradual changes in the conceptualization and treatment of children. The success of women's liberation, the sexual revolution, and civil rights movements hinged on raising the next generation in radically different ways. The counterculture movements of the 1960s were youth movements made possible by profound changes in parenting in the post-war period, changes motivated by a recognition that strict, dehumanizing parenting plays a significant role in the rise of fascism. The responsibility of the activist, then, is to unburden children from the cultural artifices that have sedimented over millennia, allowing children the opportunity to remake the world. It is not the responsibility of the adult to fantasize about a future but to prepare the world by *childing* the present. Futurism is an abandonment of the present and of intergenerational justice, an imaginative colonization of the world that can only be created by subsequent generations. It is incumbent on adults to promote conditions under which the child can be equipped and secure enough to remake the world. If we fail to acknowledge the intergenerational nature of social change, collective decision making will remain the exclusive purview of adults, according to the forms of agency privileged by adults, denied to the young and anyone else categorized as frozen in childhood, to the exclusion of all else.

The Children of Children: Why the Adultification Thesis is a Misguided Trap for Black Children and Families

By Stacey Patton

I am a journalist and child advocate who has spent the past fifteen years obsessively trying to convince Black people to stop whupping children because it is one of the whitest things that parents and caretakers can do to inadvertently sabotage the developmental trajectories of our children. Whuppings undermine the health and future potential of our communities, perpetuate anti-Blackness, and assist the reproduction of white supremacist violence, which helps to produce the very docility, trauma, and negative public-health outcomes required to sustain the racial order. In the world of science, medicine, and child advocacy, we are witnessing growing attention to health disparities associated with maltreatment and toxic stress in childhood, along with global campaigns to end corporal punishment in schools and at home. Physical punishment erodes children's self-esteem and health over their lifespan, their sense of bodily integrity and dignity, forces them to accept violence as normal, and to demand respect through aggression.

In the United States, physical punishment is routinely practiced by upwards of 70 percent of Black parents, even though it remains the number one risk factor for abuse.[1] Not surprisingly, the top ten paddling states, where disproportionate numbers of Black children are routinely hit with paddles by teachers and administrators at higher rates than their white peers, were also the top ten lynching states in the early-twentieth century.[2]

---

1   Stacey Patton, "Stop Beating Black Children," *New York Times*, March 10, 2017.

2   Stacey Patton, *Spare the Kids: Why Whupping Children Won't Save Black America* (Boston: Beacon Press, 2017).

In the grim calculus of Black life, the number of young lives lost is staggering. Between 2009 and 2019, a total of 4,298 Black children in the United States died as a result of maltreatment, according to annual statistics gathered by the National Child Abuse and Neglect Data System. Around 40 percent of those fatalities were a result of physical punishment, and Black children are killed at a rate two to three times higher than their white counterparts.[3] Beating, spanking, whupping—whatever semantics you want to use to describe hitting—are all a form of internalized racism and "white body supremacy," and an intergenerational re-enactment of the violence of slavery, Jim Crow terrorism, and contemporary state-sanctioned serial killings of Black adults and youths.[4]

Corporal punishment is a continuation of a long heritage of childism and ritualistic anti-child violence that can be traced back to Europe, where it has been a tradition since at least the Middle Ages, sustained by intergenerational trauma that showed up centuries later in colonized Black parenting traditions.[5] America's white supremacist racial order fundamentally relies on fear and pain to shape the subjectivities of Black people during childhood, whether that violence is exercised by white police officers and racist vigilantes or by community proxies such as Black parents and teachers. Black parenting culture has in many ways internalized the view that corporal punishment is required to instill Black youth with the discipline necessary to protect them against police violence, mass incarceration, and pernicious forms of "adultification" bias in schools and other child-focused institutional settings.

For much of my activist life I have explained that the harsh punishment experienced by Black children within their families has been in response to living in a racist country that continues to deny our young access to the privileges and protections of the "sacred" space of childhood. I consistently made the argument in national print and broadcast outlets, in keynote speeches, community gatherings, and trainings with child welfare and juvenile justice

---

3   U.S. Department of Health and Human Services, Administration for Children and Families, Children's Bureau (2009–2019) "Child maltreatment," https://www.acf.hhs.gov/cb/research-data-technology/statistics-research/child-maltreatment.

4   On "white body supremacy," see Resmaa Menakem, *My Grandmother's Hands: Racialized Trauma and the Pathway to Mending Our Hearts and Bodies* (Las Vegas: Central Recovery Press, 2017).

5   For a good discussion on "childism," see Elisabeth Young-Bruehl, *Childism: Confronting Prejudice Against Children* (New Haven: Yale University Press, 2013).

professionals that the acceleration of Black children into perceived maturity has long been a hallmark of anti-Blackness in America.[6]

But I was wrong.

I have not been alone in perpetuating this misguided thinking about the age compression of Black children and all of its insidious consequences. Many other activists, political commentators, academics, and policymakers have advanced the adultification bias thesis through quantitative and qualitative studies on the experiences of Black children and through surveys of racial attitudes. Scholars and commentators have argued that there is a deliberate unwillingness to see Black youth as children. That popular conceptions on what it means to be a child and who gets to be a child are structured against Black children. That Black children are pathologized as angry, disrespectful, sassy, deviant, threatening, criminal, sexually precocious, and carry adult-like culpability. And that Black children are denied empathy, compassion, nurturance, and opportunities to learn from their mistakes like their white peers.[7]

"People of all races see black children as less innocent, more adultlike and more responsible for their actions than their white peers," historian Robin Bernstein wrote in a 2017 commentary for the New York Times titled, "Let Black Kids Just Be Kids." She added, "normal childhood behavior, like disobedience, tantrums and back talk, is seen as a criminal threat when black kids do it. Social scientists have found that this misperception causes black children to be pushed out, overpoliced and underprotected."[8]

When sixteen-year-old Ma'Khia Bryant, a former foster youth from

---

6   See, for example, Stacey Patton, "In America, Black Children Don't Get to Be Children," *Washington Post*, November 26, 2014.

7   Rebecca Epstein, Jamilia J. Blake, and Thalia González, *Girlhood Interrupted: The Erasure of Black Girls' Childhood*, Georgetown Law Center on Poverty and Inequality, July 18, 2017; "What Went Wrong: Analysis of Police Handcuffing, Pepper-Spraying 9-Year-Old Girl," NPR Special Series: *America Reckons with Racial Injustice*, March 9, 2021; D.L. Bernard, C.D. Calhoun, D.E. Banks, C.A. Halliday, C. Hughes-Halbert, and C.K. Danielson, "Making the 'C-ACE' for a Culturally-Informed Adverse Childhood Experiences Framework to Understand the Pervasive Mental Health Impact of Racism on Black Youth," *Journal of Child & Adolescent Trauma* 14 (2), 233–47; Walter S. Gilliam, Angela N. Maupin, Chin R. Reyes, Maria Accavitti, and Frederick Shic, "Do Early Educators' Implicit Biases Regarding Sex and Race Relate to Behavior Expectations and Recommendations of Preschool Expulsions and Suspensions?" Yale University Child Study Center, September 2016; American Psychological Association, "Black Boys Viewed as Older, Less Innocent Than Whites Research Finds" [Press release], March 6, 2014, http://www.apa.org/news/press/releases/2014/03/black-boys-older.

8   Robin Bernstein, "Let Black Kids Just Be Kids," *New York Times*, July 26, 2017.

Columbus, Ohio, was killed in April 2021 by a police officer, a number of Black feminist commentators invoked adultification bias to explain why she and other Black youth are more frequently killed than their white peers by police. A *New York Times* article noted that Bryant was consistently referred to as a "young woman" and depicted as a plus-sized, uncontrollable threat that could only be contained with lethal force.

Dr. Jamilia Blake, a psychology professor at Texas A&M and coauthor of a popular 2017 report "Girlhood Interrupted" (cited above) on the erasure of Black girlhood, echoed Cooper's sentiments. She told the *New York Times* that Black girls are not seen as innocent, are not afforded the ability to make mistakes or given the benefit of doubt, and adultification bias may be driving the severity of punitive responses against them by teachers, mental health providers, and law enforcement.[9]

"How it looks in school is this general perception of Black girls' behavior being very volitional and menacing, and even more so if they voice their concerns and raise awareness—everything that they do is kind of seen as problematic. They are constantly monitored, they receive more severe disciplinary actions, and they aren't even able to be sad or cry," Blake said.[10]

Monique Morris, president and chief executive of Grantmakers for Girls of Color and author of *Pushout: The Criminalization of Black Girls in School*, echoed Blake by saying the age compression of adultification is "a way to erase the normal adolescent behavior and development that we have come to associate with young people … it heightens our propensity to respond to young people as if they're fully developed adults—referring to girls as women, not allowing them to make mistakes, even [affects] how we define their responses to conditions."[11]

It took a fellow academic friend, Toby Rollo,[12] whose research focuses on conceptions of childhood and political theory, to help me see how problematic these studies are because of their methodological flaws and because they reinforce the idea that there's some general societal protection of children that then perpetuates a perverse misunderstanding of white supremacy as child-friendly

---

9   Alisha Haridasani Gupta, "'More than Just Tragic': Ma'khia Bryant and the Burden of Black Girlhood," *New York Times*, April 24, 2021, https://www.nytimes.com/2021/04/24/us/makhia-bryant.html.

10   Ibid.

11   Ibid.

12   Toby Rollo is a political science professor at Lakehead University in Ontario, Canada, and writes extensively about this topic.

for some children. The adultification thesis gets things backwards partly because it relies too heavily on popular representations of protected "childhood inno- cence" rather than on the actual histories and experiences of children. Rollo invited me to start reading more about the history of white children's traumatic experiences in European cultures and how that abuse set the behavioral patterns of their descendants, who would then displace their unhealed trauma, rage, and barbarism onto people of color around the globe, through colonization, enslave- ment, apartheid, and other forms of state violence.

In reality, the history of childhood in the west is a dark and brutal story of mistreatment, sexualization, and murder.[13] Even when children were viewed as "innocent" it was a curse. The celebration of childhood innocence in art and culture has obscured the fact that childhood in the west has always been an exceedingly unsafe and violent phase of life, even today. Once I started get- ting deeper into the archives, I began to see that white people modeled their treatment of Black people on their barbaric treatment of their own children. Through colonization and enslavement, Black people became white people's new children.

Today, popular thinking says that only white youth are allowed to be chil- dren. Educators and law enforcement treat Black children more like adults, which is supposed to explain away the denial of innocence and protection that they experience. The idea that the perpetual discrimination and dispropor- tionate violence against Black children happens because they are being adul- tified is a sign that we are holding on to a false premise that racism, and all of its wicked intergenerational sadism, will stop with children. But the deliberate targeting and destruction of children is a white supremacist fail-safe mecha- nism and an essential strategy for its self-protection. Black children are and have always been a threat to the continuity of white supremacy, and conse- quently have been treated as enemy combatants in the same brutal manner as their elders.

In America, Black children experience disproportionate levels of abuse and murder precisely because they are Black and because they are children, not because they are being expedited into adulthood. In the racist mindset, Black children are considered the children of children, doubly doomed by their categorization as biological children as well as offspring of an inferior race existing in a permanent condition of cultural infancy, lawlessness, and criminality, for whom coercive punishment and death are the law's only recourse. As my fellow academic friend, Toby Rollo, has explained in his own

---

13   Lloyd deMause, ed., *The History of Childhood* (New York: Harper & Row, 1975).

research, childhood in the west has always been a site of naturalized violence in social, legal, and political culture. It is considered a stage of irrationality and lawlessness that requires coercive and sometimes deadly discipline to maintain order. According to Rollo, "To be labelled infantile, childish, or childlike is the ultimate disqualification to participate in the safe and secure domain of exclusive adult privilege. This logic is then applied to other groups in order to racialize them, leading to the disqualification of Black, Indigenous, and other peoples as members of the immature and irrational 'child-races.'"[14]

The formerly enslaved and famous abolitionist Frederick Douglass understood that the insidious nature of white supremacy denied adulthood to actual Black adult bodies and to children evolving into adult bodies. He observed in *My Bondage and My Freedom*, written in 1855, that white youth were permitted to graduate into citizens, leaving behind the degraded powerless condition of youth. Writing on the maturing of Tommy, his childhood companion and master, he said: "He could grow and become a MAN; I could grow, though I could not become a man, but must remain, all my life, a minor—a mere boy."[15] Here, Douglass articulated the deep logic of white supremacy: the dehumanization and enslavement of Black people through their designation as permanent children dependent upon the "benevolence" and civilizing hand of slave-owners.

Douglass's insight tells us that infantilization already set Black people up for discrimination and violence. In a white-supremacist society, there can be no mature Black people. They are always children. Which means that adultification would have the opposite effect of undoing infantilization and liberating Black people. Which means we must ask: if white supremacy is an attempt to undo the view that Black people can be adults, at least in potential, what, then, would be the point of adultifying Black children?

Meanwhile, white youth are treated better because they are conceptualized as quasi-adults, not children. Since the late-nineteenth century, white youth have been increasingly spared the risks of childhood through their recategorization as would-be adults and future citizens. For example, the juvenile justice system emerged at the turn of the century as part of the

---

14 Toby Rollo, "Feral Children: Settler Colonialism, Progress, and the Figure of the Child," *Settler Colonial Studies* 8, no. 1 (2018):60–79; and "The Color of Childhood: The Role of the Child/Human Binary in the Production of Anti-Black Racism," *Journal of Black Studies* 49, no. 4 (2018): 307–29.

15 Frederick Douglass, *My Bondage and My Freedom* (New York: Miller, Orton & Mulligan, 1855), 328.

burgeoning child-saving movement, which included orphanages and schools. These institutions were established in the way of Black Emancipation to elevate white children out of the experiences of poverty and abuse, which they shared with newly freed Black children, much to the dismay of white society. White children were removed from the degraded category of childhood in order to preserve the future of white nationalism. They were reconceptualized as reformable, as future citizens, and they partially benefitted from adult freedoms and privileges such as the legal presumption of innocence. Whereas Black people are perpetual children, there is no such thing as a white child. White youth are always already "future adults," and adulthood represents the archetype of full humanity from which Black people are permanently excluded. Black youth, in contrast, will remain perpetual children—lawless and ungovernable.

From this historical perspective, we see that Black youth have never been and are not being denied childhood. Rather, they are the victims of the category of childhood that has long existed as a space of exploitation and brutality. The same is true of Black people more generally. Age is a moot point. Dominant racist narratives have always infantilized Black people, referring to them as a "child race" and conceptualizing them as perpetual children. It is not a trivial fact, for when Black people are defined as children, it naturalizes and therefore justifies the cruelties of slavery, segregation, mass incarceration, and police brutality.

One of the first steps in decolonizing Black parenting is to reframe our understanding of the conception of childhood. Childhood in America and throughout the western world has never been a protected category. It is a perennial site of violence. For a thousand years at least, white people have used trauma through corporal punishment, toxic religiosity, treating children as property, and exposing them to public terror to actualize and ensure the future of white supremacy. The fact is that white supremacy requires the destruction of ALL children in myriad ways so that they grow up to underwrite the logics and horrors of racism. Adultification, by contrast, is actually protective because being an adult is a privileged position. The reason white youth are more protected is because they are treated like adults—they benefit from adultification. When Black youth are targeted for violence, it is precisely because they are children. When Black adults are targeted for violence, it is, once again, because they are conceptualized as children.

What does all this mean for Black parenting?

We need to decolonize our Black parenting. This means that we must understand how our parenting practices have been formed by systems of oppression, which affects not only how parents think about and relate to their children but also to themselves. It means that we must understand how toxic European concepts about childhood and practices toward children were absorbed into our traditions to the degree that we believe they are natural and even intrinsic to our own culture. Decolonization also invites us to understand that white supremacy fundamentally depends on Black parental coercion and violence against children in order to reproduce itself so that we raise generations of broken and traumatized children who will project their trauma and rage back onto themselves and communities rather than our oppressors.

We should not be treating our children as though they have the same emotional responsibility as adults and be held accountable as such. We should not be acting as though children's motivations and thought processes are the same as adults, which then justifies applying adult consequences. I work with so many Black parents and caregivers who ignore developmental processes or how the brain and nervous system works from infancy to age twenty-four. They do not have developmentally appropriate expectations for their children or respect that children and adults don't interpret actions and consequences in the same way. By using trauma as a form of love and protection, far too many Black caregivers are complicit in the very destruction of our children that we are trying to prevent. Quite frankly, Black children's first experiences with the denial of innocence comes from within families where they are called "bad" and "fast" and are subjected to other demonizing labels starting in early childhood.

The question is not "Are our children seen as children in this culture?" but "Have Black people, irrespective of age, ever been conceptualized as adults?" Those of us who are activists and advocates should not be arguing that Black children should be treated as children. But rather, we should all become advocates for the empowerment and humanization of children. Child advocacy is Black liberation work. And Black liberation work must include child advocacy.

It is only by fully understanding the true roots and history of the European views and treatment of white children and their relationship to the formation and sustenance of systemic anti-Black racism that we can genuinely understand and begin to address how Black children are viewed and treated, especially within Black families, institutions, and communities. We need to recognize how childism is harming, traumatizing, and even killing Black children—too often at the hands of the Black adults entrusted with their lives. And we absolutely must move beyond the current practice of mis-labeling the reasons for so many forms of abuse suffered by Black children as adultification. The actual truth is far more dangerous and disturbing: that Black youth cannot ever be allowed the full agency of political or social adulthood because that would challenge white supremacist control. It's time for Black adults to trade in the adultification theory for the realities of childism.

There are no perfect victims in a white supremacist culture. But we can free ourselves, one child at a time. And when we exorcise the pain and rage, we will discover that other emotions and liberating possibilities will spring forward.[16]

---

16 Supplemental materials: Jacqueline Douge, "Disciplining Our Children with Dr. Stacey Patton," *What is Black* podcast, https://podcasts.apple.com/us/podcast/part-1-disciplining-our-children-with-dr-stacey-patton/id1448214889?i=1000430095776. "Corporal punishment not intrinsic to Black culture," American Psychological Association, https://www.apa.org/pi/families/resources/newsletter/2017/04/racial-trauma. "Stop Beating Black Children," *New York Times*, March 10, 2017, https://www.nytimes.com/2017/03/10/opinion/sunday/stop-beating-black-children.html. "Why Is America Celebrating the Beating of a Black Child?" *Washington Post*, April 29, 2015, https://www.washingtonpost.com/posteverything/wp/2015/04/29/why-is-america-celebrating-the-beating-of-a-black-child.

"Blah Blah Blah" No Longer: Learning to Host, Celebrate, and Follow a New Generation

By Gustavo Esteva, Madhu S. Prakash, and Dana L. Stuchul

Three generations ago, Gandhi spoke a vision of leadership whose challenge we'd be wise to heed: "There goes my people. I must follow them, for I am their leader." Today, the young declare "No more blah blah blah."[1] Bequeathed violent legacies yielding cultural, climatic, economic, social, linguistic, and vernacular destruction, the young now mobilize hope as a social force, re-thinking and re-making our worlds. With clear vision, they see what is wrong and what has failed. Eschewing naiveté, they actively cast off old constructs and strictures, broken promises, and failed premises undergirding the worlds into which they've been born. Among these are classifications such as *infant* (etymologically, "non-speaker") from which a host of hierarchical impositions and separations have followed. In this way, they are co-creating convivial and hope-filled possibilities, "beyond blah blah blah."

Since its invention, "childhood" has had unfortunate repercussions. Ushering in a new social order—the dominance of capital—the invention of childhood transmogrified the young into "children," requiring new treatments (compulsory education) and new social expectations (the consumption of schooling for social legitimacy). To be viewed as worthy of full inclusion and participation within the social order, the "not yet," the less than full humans (a contemporary manifestation of earlier and oppressive hierarchies, e.g. barbarians, savages, infidels, underdeveloped, and uneducated) would require treatments, discipline, and control. To learn new ways of seeing the young, to recognize them as full human beings, whose inclusion and participation within

---

1 Greta Thunberg in the COP 26 Conference in Glasgow, Scotland.

the social whole is valued, requires abandoning all those ideas that diminish and deny their full humanity—beginning with the category of "childhood."

In this book, various writers share their reflections on how to interact with children in more creative and just ways. Challenging principles of obedience and submission—those fundamental rules of the modern nation-state—authors share accounts of different forms of interaction among "adults" and "youth," freed from patterns of dominance, control, obedience, and submission, those enshrined within schooling. Bearing witness to how both climate and institutional collapse renders contemporary knowledge and practices useless or worse (an extension of violence), authors explore new ways of engagement with new attitudes, appropriate for a world that is dying and being re-generated.

To be sure, our current predicaments lay bare a new world barely recognizable. The crises—really opportunities—present the moment for abandoning the pernicious compulsion to "prepare the new generation for the future." All manner of "future" ideology—a conservative, if not reactionary, position—rationalizes acting today as if "the future" can be known. Rather, today's myriad of uncertainties offers extraordinary possibilities to learn, together with young people, how to live in this new world, and how to construct it differently.

Let's imagine a world in which those just born are received and perceived with wonder. Imagine honoring and respecting them as full and whole human beings, rather than deficient or less than, as weak and needing manipulation and control. Imagine a world in which we learn with them—as they and we grow—how to create a world constructed on the awareness that we are all indelibly, inextricably, and inseparably *of* Mother Earth. Imagine, therefore, behaving in every interaction and in every exchange, acting to do everything humanly possible to preserve, protect, nurture, and strengthen our Mother; a world in which we continually practice relatedness, not separation. Imagine that instead of sacrificing the infinite curiosity of young people, their incredible passion for learning, on the altar of imposed teachings, we learn from the newly born to resist all manner of authoritarianism and patriarchy—to learn within the world what is needed to live well, today.

For too long, beneath the banner of "childhood," many have assumed and imposed an artificial existence onto the young. "Needing" to be prepared prior to assuming their places within the "adult" world, "needing" to be protected from the cruelties of adult interactions, "needing" to be controlled and manipulated, "children" have been set apart. Assuming their "ignorance," their deficiencies, we have extended the artificiality of their existence, separating them from meaning, from meaningful engagement with the world as it is.

From the time a newly born person enters the world, they are immediately reduced, forced to conform to the prevailing mold as a self(ish), narcissistic, individual—separate from others. As they grow, they are too soon robbed of their capacities to love and to learn within their communities. The goal: to be competitive individuals as soon as possible. To be "educated" is to be processed for removal from one's community, to assert one's individual pursuits, toward ever new forms of consumption. However, the brutal individualism currently plaguing modern societies is not natural to newborns. It has a beginning and can similarly have an ending.

The time is now to end the dehumanizing hierarchies, patronizing, and patriarchal attitudes embedded within the categories of childhood. What's more, matriarchal traditions offer hopeful alternatives: the delights in the wonder of new life; knowing that each being has arrived to flow in ways we cannot know or predict. As Kahlil Gibran observed, "You may give them your love, but not your thoughts. For they have their own thoughts."[2]

In many parts of the Global South, mothers still perform all their daily activities carrying their babies on their backs, inside their *rebozos*. This practice, which may last for many months, gives the babies the opportunity to participate in all activities and thus begin authentic and sustained interaction with the world in which they are entering. Here they are known as part of a "we," rather than as an "I." Freed from the need for achievement, for proving one's worthiness in endless cycles of consumption and competition, the baby grows in awareness that to be human is to be "knots in nets of relationships."

Years ago, Zapatista Comandante Tacho said, "listening is not just to hear the other, but to be ready to be transformed by the other."[3] When we listen and hear, when we look and see each other—with deepest respect—we recognize in "the other," a part of our own being that we do not yet know. The seeds of a convivial society are thus sown.

In a convivial society, we interact with others by looking and listening to the person in front of us, in their singular and unique condition, instead of confronting them with the filter of some classification, according to age, gender, profession, or activity. This can be particularly important for the so-called child, always seen from the superior position of adulthood.

Infants may require instruction for simple acts: brushing teeth, taking baths, swimming in safe waters before venturing further, but they learn by

---

2   Kahlil Gibran, "On Children," in *The Prophet* (New York: Alfred A. Knopf, 1923), 8–9. References are to line.

3   Juan Mayorga, *Aprender en libertad* (Universidad de la Tierra, México: Albora, 2020).

themselves, through simple interaction, to walk, speak, and think, some of the most complex things we do. In homes with many siblings, the youngest learn organically and simply, yearning to practice with joy what their elders are thoroughly enjoying. They don't need to be taught joy in being alive. They are born of it. Joy abounds when they are protected from imposing orders and can rejoice with invitations to explore the magical world around them; to consider options and different sources of inspiration, knowledge, or wisdom—what the trees or the ants do, what ancient peoples did, what we did before technologies rendered our senses useless. Let's assume for a moment that instead of sharing with them our habits, prejudices, and modes of perception, the newly born learn in freedom. They get care and love instead of "education," the endeavor to shape them in a certain way. With an open imagination, the young may try to create new ways of living, ways not limited to the prevailing, soul-crushing and violent narratives dominating what it means to be alive.

Discovering the realities of the world alongside younger people, who are generally free from the prejudices that life itself accumulates in all people through experience, has more foundation than ever. Many routines still persist. The same old things are repeated. But it is increasingly necessary to be open to surprise. In the past, it was possible to anticipate events with reasonable accuracy because there were deep trends that allowed us to foresee the evolution of most of those events in daily life. These trends have disappeared. Climate and socio-political collapse have led us to radical uncertainty. No one can know with reasonable certainty what is going to happen. The climate we had is gone and we know very little about the one emerging. At every corner we hear: "This has never happened before"; "It's not raining this month"; "We have May temperatures when it's October"... Things are even more uncertain in the social and political world. Nobody knows. Instead of dogmatically explaining to younger people how things are and will be, we can share with them our uncertainties and explore with them what we will experience and can create. Hopefully, we will soon discover that, instead of needing our guidance, we can create a new world together, with their inspiration and imagination.

A new generation is already enraged with the disaster we created and are transforming their dignified rage into magnificent militancy to do what needs to be done. "No more blah blah blah," said Greta Thunberg in the COP 26 Conference in Glasgow. "No more exploitation of people, nature and the planet."[4]

---

4   "Greta Thunberg on COP26: 'No More Blah Blah Blah,'" YouTube video, https://www .youtube.com/watch?v=C2ekjFt6J4A.

She is not alone in her rebellion. She is just the symptom and expression of a wide phenomenon. Most of these young rebels started with a concern about climate collapse, which they already felt in the skin, but soon included social issues. Like adults, they looked to the top, presenting their claims to governments and corporations, but they got tired of the reaction they received. They did not go to Glasgow to present demands to the big and the powerful. They went to listen to each other and weave agreements to act. Fifteen brilliant Indigenous women, for example, in the name of their organization, Indigenous Futures, sent a clear message: "Those inside the Conference should learn to silence and listen. Simulation should stop. We don't need development. We know how to live in our territories." "We did not come to talk to the powerful," said Mitzi Cortés, a young Mixtec from Oaxaca, Mexico. "We came to articulate ourselves with other struggles. Change will come from below, not from the top, from the leaders of the world."[5]

Greta started her campaign when she was eight years old. There are many like her. The sisters Isabel and Melati Wilsen were less than twelve years old when they started their campaign against plastics in Bali, Indonesia. Avery McRae is the second youngest in a group of twelve youth that presented a demand against the US government for its responsibility in the climate collapse. Re Cabrera also started in primary school, linking gender and climate struggles. In 2019, she participated in the organization of the Third World Climate Strike. At nineteen years old, Re came to Glasgow to continue her struggle against racism and patriarchy.

To reforest hearts and territories, Indigenous women organized a very special event: "A cura da Terra." Governments and corporations, they said, "want to prescribe the same medicine: green capitalism; inclusive colonialism; sustainable development; recycled extractivism." They knew how to heal territories and spirits, "real, living solutions to climate crisis," and assumed the responsibility "to continue breathing life; to continue weaving among Indigenous women; to continue creating healing spaces to end the inequality which is the very root of the crisis."

"Survival of the human race depends of the rediscovery of hope as a social force," wrote Ivan Illich fifty years ago.[6] In streets all over the world, not only in Glasgow, young people, mainly women, are illustrating today how they are rediscovering hope and already transforming it into a powerful social force. That is what the Zapatistas encountered during their trip to "Rebellious Land," as

---

5   Gustavo Esteva, "El gran viraje," *La Jornada*, November 15, 2021.

6   Ivan Illich, *Deschooling Society* (London: Marion Boyars, 1972), 106.

they baptized Europe: a new hope that those already constructing a new world are formulating, laughing at those that continue with their blah blah blah.

The time has come to celebrate with children and youth; to accept their guidance and inspiration; to lead by following them. We must do so as if all our lives depend upon it. They do.

Fire of Ata: The Raging Voice is a Song of Love

By Gabriel Zacuto

Teaching the innate

We are always learning. This process need not be arranged, managed, or coerced. Not any more than a healthy heart must be forced to beat. This is especially true for the young, and yet we put considerable effort, wealth, and time into inculcating children with what we expect them to know and believe. The joke is on us though, because despite the outsized influence of parents and educators, we cannot truly choose who our children are or who they will be. Who they become is partially dependent on the social world they emerge from, but it is more a matter of reflection than dictation.

Whether we understand it as socialization or social control, the greater part of childrearing, whether at home or school, is dedicated to behavior modification. The notion that children should cooperate, on demand, at least within immediate social groups, is universal, and the consensus seems to be that this must be taught through admonition, punishment, or reward.

Schooling, which nearly all children are subjected to, is founded upon individual achievement. From kindergarten to university, one of the greatest transgressions consists in aiding others through the unauthorized sharing of information. In other situations however, we insist that children must share. The subtext being that they should share within their families, teams, and peer groups. Sharing beyond those borders is likely to conjure the specter of wealth redistribution, much feared by the ruling classes who set the ideological tone of society.

Our pedagogy is as contradictory as the social order itself. Children must learn to share but also to accumulate. They must embody traditional values but think freely as individuals. Value justice but ignore oppression. Seek peace but enact violence. Follow laws that are universally transgressed, adapted to suit corporate interests and selectively punished. Ironically, the children of wealthy countries are regarded as more "free" than adults, but are expected to spend the majority of their time completing the tasks of schooling.

If cooperation is framed as a virtue, and encouraged by liberal pedagogies, then it is always against the backdrop of the competitive mode that our present society is structured upon. In liberal, market-based systems, competition is often described as a fraught but unavoidable aspect of human nature, and in the next breath defended as a virtue that brings about freedom, innovation, and affordable goods. In practice, all competition guarantees is inequality and violence. Nevertheless, the majority of parents, educators, and politicians believe that competition builds character, grit, resilience, and independence in children. The same rationale has been used as an apologia for corporal punishment. Competition is thus nurtured and naturalized.

And what is the moral of this story?

William Golding's 1954 novel *Lord of the Flies*, a staple of high school reading lists, eloquently describes the predicament of a group of English schoolboys who become stranded on an uninhabited island. The boys form relationships and rituals that establish a tentative social order, but as the novel progresses, conflicts between the characters grow and their interactions become unstable, violent, and finally, deadly. Eventually, they are found and rescued by British naval officers.

Golding's intention was apparently to present a realistic account of human behavior. The novel is generally understood in the Hobbesian sense, which suggests that left to their own devices, people are self-interested, power seeking, and competitive. Golding told of children who, removed from the civilizing influence of authority, revert to a brutal existence that would presumably have led to all their deaths had they not been rescued by military emissaries of a colonial power already so well known as "civilizers" of island nations. Of course, by *civilization*, I mean enslavement and genocide.

Dutch historian Rutger Bregman recently unearthed a true account that closely parallels Golding's story. In 1965, a group of six boys between the ages of thirteen and sixteen escaped from a Catholic boarding school in Tonga, stole a boat, and set out hoping to reach Fiji or New Zealand. The boat soon became damaged and the boys were adrift for days before reaching a small rocky island, Ata, which had been stripped of its Indigenous inhabitants by slave traders a hundred years earlier.

The boys were discovered fifteen months later by Peter Warner, the wayfaring son of an Australian industrialist, who happened to be sailing nearby. These events closely parallel the plot and setting of Golding's novel, though what actually took place on Ata diverges entirely from that fictional account. On the island, the boys established what their rescuer described as a small commune where they kept a garden, animals, stores of food and water, and a fire that they kept perpetually burning. The boys collectively assigned duties and worked in teams to do the necessary work of survival. When conflicts arose, they used a scheme that allowed time apart so tempers could cool. During their time on the island, one boy suffered a broken leg, but rather than this leading to his doom, the other boys assumed their injured comrade's duties and allowed him to rest for weeks while his body healed. When the boys were eventually picked up by Warner, they were all in excellent physical condition.

Conventional wisdom holds Golding's parable as a great exemplar of the competitive, Hobbesian understanding of children's and, therefore, human behavior. The empirical, true account is more in line with the cooperative tendency that Russian anarchist luminary Peter Kropotkin termed "mutual aid."

Mutual aid refers to the inherent tendency of living beings to help one another, acting in the interest of both the individual and collective good. As understood socially, the deliberate enactment of mutual aid represents the only set of practices that can both reduce our dependence on the existing power structure and also address our immediate material needs. Wherever life exists, both competitive and cooperative relationships are possible. One great lie perpetuated within hierarchical societies, and especially via liberal theory, is that competition is a naturally dominant tendency.

This elides the history of Empire, through which competition has become dominant through violence, discipline, and acculturation. These hierarchic relations have not brought about a straightforward replacement of cooperation by competition. Oppressive systems such as ours have always held power through the deliberate conjunction of the cooperative and competitive modes, which, in applications, allows the oppressed to be turned against one another. In short, cooperation has been subsumed by what I call *cooperative exclusion*.

United we stand divided

At the dinner table we pass the salt. In the corporate world, we pour salt in the wound. We give the next door neighbor a cup of sugar but call the police on the homeless denizen, who is seen as deserving of the needless suffering they endure. We scoop pollution from duck ponds, then drink privatized water from plastic bottles made from petroleum, robbed from native lands, and destined to befoul Earth's oceans. The desire for collective good has been wedded to the commodification of all life. Cooperation and competition are conjoined in struggle.

While teams, nations, and social classes militate against one another, internal cooperation is generally encouraged. Children cooperate with teammates to defeat the opposition. Employees pull together to destroy the competition. Police and soldiers walk in lockstep over the bodies of protestors, protectors, and everyday people. This mode of social interaction is not specific to schooling, sports, boardrooms, or the military. Cooperative exclusion is quintessential to the ideology of liberalism and its attendant deity, the free market, which far from being a truly laissez faire institution is continually nurtured and rescued by the "invisible hand" of the state.

One of the most pervasive and deliberate forms of cooperative exclusion in the west, and especially in so-called North America manifests in the form of racism. The socially constructed and ever-evolving category of whiteness has deliberately been propagated by the ruling classes. It functions to grant relative privilege to those considered white, in order to sever ties with other racialized groups. Through relative privilege and the perceived threat of the other, a false, racist solidarity emerges that only strengthens the position of those who exploit those of all races. Cooperative bonds within the dominant group are strengthened and war is waged upon the oppressed. When Western states are able to stabilize their markets and keep growth high, we see another form of exclusion. This one, a sacred cow of "progressive" liberals. Social Democracy is a form of political economy that specifically champions egalitarianism and the liberty (of markets). To the extent that it succeeds in establishing high standards of living for the citizens of specific nation states, it does so only by depriving workers and citizens of poor, formerly colonized nations the same rights and wealth.

The majority of adults (and in poor nations, many children) spend most of their waking hours engaged in waged labor. The workplace is a quintessential site of cooperative exclusion as well as individualized competition. Schooling, like waged labor, relies on those innate cooperative capacities that have been subsumed by the regime of capitalism and the competitive social relations it necessitates.

Theorists across the ideological spectrum, from Althusser to Illich, have described schooling as a site of ideological indoctrination. The state seeks to maintain stability and capital accumulation, uses schooling to inculcate a particular system of knowledge and understanding of time and work discipline to produce a compliant citizenry and workforce. Those who are deemed superfluous, or noncompliant, are ejected from the system and largely relegated to lives of desperation and incarceration. This group is ever growing and always coded by class and race.

Schooling also serves a custodial function that reinforces indoctrination, allows for continuity with the carceral system, and most obviously, allows the parents of students the "free" time to be exploited members of the same workforce that their children, if "successful," are soon to join. Schooling deliberately disrupts open exploration and play, and promulgates cooperative exclusion through organized sports. Ivan Illich put it well in his 1971 book, *Deschooling Society*: the "games" of the physical education department "take the form of warlike tournaments...[and they] have undermined the playfulness of sports and are used to reinforce the competitive nature of schools."[1]

So how can we reach for worlds where the needs of all are addressed collectively and individuals are allowed to grow, create, and love, free of cages and the imposition of power? There is no single answer to this question but it's clear that only the full expression of mutual aid can allow us to challenge the dominance of the states that preserve the function of capitalism. The problem we face is that our tendency toward mutual aid has been subsumed by cooperative exclusion. Most of us spend all our time working, lost in fantasy worlds or other private pursuits, and reserve the energy we have left to offer aid to those we know and love best. It is essential that we transcend this system.

The reason this society places such importance on the inculcation of youth was never so they might learn to work together cooperatively. Young people cannot simply be trusted to obey orders. They must be made to do so. So we teach them to join teams within teams within teams. Entire industries and manifold institutions must be dedicated to their indoctrination, lest they grow to demand the collective liberation that power fears. They are simultaneously the greatest asset and most dire threat to the status quo.

---

1   Ivan Illich, *Deschooling Society* (New York: Harper & Row, 1971), 58.

Toward the flame

This liberation is already happening, every day. Not all at once, but through what John Holloway called "cracks" in hierarchical, racial capitalism, which have not been fully colonized by the brutality of quantitative reasoning and the drive to accumulation.[2] The spirit of youth and refusal will split this monolithic world apart and build new ones in its place where the desire to live cooperatively in mutual support and interdependent autonomy is not turned against itself and twisted up with Empire. If this planet and its people are to live on, we must let youth destroy who we are today.

Cracks exist in a nascent stage within families, teams, parties, and nations. Empire tells us to look within the group, but each of us is potentially a seed, which under the proper conditions can take root and spread a wide and embracing love made flesh through mutualistic practice. The love between family members is thought of as qualitatively different from radical love but it has the same essence, and once set free from the constraint that liberal capitalism imposes, it will be that seed. We in the West have been inculcated with the neoliberal notion that people in need are deserving of starvation, and even the use of state welfare, if available, is to be condemned as a type of theft. In reality the needy have been parasitized by owners and bosses, and removed from institutional logic. We all know this.

Poor and working people have always shared with one another. If nothing else, necessity accounts for this, though these practices are an inheritance of all life forms, independent of species or station. Mutual aid, as opposed to charity, welfare, and subsistence on wages is a form of support that cannot be withheld by the power structure. When we help ourselves, we walk the road to dual power, away from the state and corporate tyranny.

Cracks also abound in the physical spaces between buildings and roads where children play. Between the hours of school and sleep, between the false and ancient names of the days of the week, across the lawns and parking lots of cities and suburbs, children lose the distinction we hold between work and play and between the collective and the individual. In play they practice skills, and learn the world. But play need not have an end. In their relationships, creativity evolves and exists for their own joy, rather than in service of the extrinsic forces of ideology and authority.

Unhindered by the capitalist tendency to recuperate and totalize, young people are practicing mutual aid with one another. Whether a matter of survival,

---

2   John Holloway, *Crack Capitalism* (London: Pluto Press, 2010).

as is often the case, or merely the expression of love between friends, children outside the reach of institutions will almost always share with one another. This makes our efforts to teach them cooperation all the more redundant and harmful. Children share their time, their laughter, and the games they invent, but when given the opportunity are equally apt to share money, food, toys, and space. Caregivers, parents, and teachers then often act as police who insist that children be less free with their possessions. There is a direct line between the liberal defense of private property and the subsumption of cooperation.

The rebellion of youth is disruptive and sometimes violent. The forces of the right often portray it as something selfish and naive. This is a lie big enough to be accepted by those ground down by capitalism, who see life on earth as a hell that no one has a right to escape except through death. But young people are competent and capable, and the rebellion of youth is more often than not thoughtful and collective in scope. When they speak out, without accommodation to years of misery, they speak to all of our better selves—versions of us not mutilated by Empire. Their raging collective voice is a song of love.

When not lashed and bound by authoritarian practice or crushed by poverty, young people are the greatest practitioners of ruthless criticism, the life blood of radical dissent. In youth, before we learn "how the world really is" and become closed to possibility, critique comes along with inquiry. The rebellions primed by the social disruptions of the pandemic and catalyzed by the murder of George Floyd were a pyroclastic flow that signaled a material rupture and a widespread shift in consciousness, particularly in young people who had been peremptorily dismissed from in-person schooling. As is usually the case during social upheavals, most of the people who occupied the streets and rallied in solidarity with Black lives and against the system were multiracial contingents of students and young adults.

What we see in every mass uprising and revolution is youth releasing the massive potentiality they carry. They refuse the burden of Atlas and tear the world apart. They determine whether this world will be reproduced or made anew. These cataclysms change the face of our world and terrify the old at heart, but they are the precursor to new worlds, just as the shattered egg opens new life. Although this destruction and renewal is the province of the chronologically young, the spirit of youth can be activated in all of us. Scientists, artists, and radicals know this. Anyone with open eyes who spends time with children sees it. When we take to the streets together to assert our solidarity, we feel it in our hearts.

My intent in writing here is not to idealize childhood or youth. Our culture already does that well enough, at least in a superficial sense. We may be ruled by old men, but the face of youth is used to launch a thousand products daily, and plastic surgery thrives. Equally, I don't want to pretend that young people can't be selfish, ignorant, and mistaken. Of course, this could describe any, if not all of us, myself included. It is our very capacity to make mistakes and continue on with youthful abandon that allows for liberatory social change.

On a personal note, welcoming my own two children into this world and caring for them continues to be the most grueling, humbling, and absolutely transcendent thing I have ever experienced. They are teaching me the true meaning of love. I believe that my personal experience is also a reflection of the universal. The emergence and growth of new life brings forth both love and conflict and only this essential conjunction can set fire to the death and stagnation that weighs so heavily upon so many of us. To stem the growth of hierarchy, that fire, like that on Ata, must be kept perpetually burning. As the line from "Solidarity Forever" proclaims, we can bring to birth a new world from the ashes of the old!

Magneto's Dreams: A New Symbol for Youth Autonomy

By carla joy bergman and Zach Bergman

"That person who helps others simply because it should or must be done, and because it is the right thing to do, is indeed without a doubt, a real superhero."
—Stan Lee, *Spiderman: Into the Spiderverse*

"The surest way to corrupt a youth is to instruct him to hold in higher esteem those who think alike than those who think differently."
—Friedrich Nietzsche, *The Dawn*

Our goal is to weave together a different kind of story about youth autonomy through our interpretation of X-Men and a couple of the characters who populate the long-running series. We focus primarily on the character of Magneto in order to discuss the nuances involved in the many forms of youth liberation movements. The X-Men story arc was centered around saving youth and protecting them from oppressive forces that seek to demean their existence, or so it seems on the surface. Of course, protecting and helping youth is wonderful, but we aim to unravel some hidden threads, perhaps even some that were in plain sight throughout X-Men, by presenting a case for Magneto as the actual symbol of liberation. Our interest in Magneto is based on the potentiality in his character, and the various symbols that were in the X-Men comics, though with less focus on the events and content in the series directly.

For the comic nerd out there, we apologize; we probably made some unfortunate leaps, but to us they made sense. Feel free to read this as fan theory, one that uses Magneto, as we see him, to symbolize a system for youth autonomy and liberation. This is a story where we all can be Magneto, and together create more thriving and justice-filled worlds.

X-Men was created by the brilliant Stan Lee and Jack Kirby, and we saw Magneto appear right out the gate in Issue #1 in 1963. Mutants are kind of super humans, all of the characters have different mutations that give them some kind of super—beyond human—power. The comic came out during a time of increasing alienation among youth, and a thriving wave of resistance to the status quo. In the comics, the mutants are often hunted and feared by other non-mutant humans. The X-Men are an elite crew of mutants under the leadership of mutant Professor Xavier, or Professor X, who works with the State to keep the world safe. Magneto, Professor X's comrade in the earlier days, saw this for what it was: a form of assimilation, so he left to create his own army of mutants. Professor Xavier's powers involve telekinesis, the ability to alter the world around him with his mind alone, which is why Magneto wears a helmet, as we discuss further below. Magneto also has the ability to alter the world itself, yet his powers are limited to the manipulation of metals. Discussing the particulars of each mutant's powers, beyond Professor Xavier and Magneto, isn't necessary.[1] But if you don't know the story of the mutants, do check it out!

carla used to be referred to as the equivalent of Professor Xavier when she worked with youth at a radical youth center in Vancouver. Being stoked with this comparison, she wore the badge with honor. We never read the X-Men comics, but we watched the cartoons and the various Marvel movies about X-Men. And given that we are both seen as outsiders (or misfits), we related to the storyline at its base level, and definitely desired a school or home where the adults would have seen us as wonderful just as we are. In the past few years, we came to recognize that the adults creating radical spaces *with* youth, including carla, were not actually Xavier, but rather a version of Magneto.

Both of us fall some place on a neuro-difference (or neuro-emergence) continuum, so we know what it feels like to be an outsider, misfit, and ostracized for being a certain way. Maybe this is why we really got into the minutiae of the X-Men story. Zach's experience is different from carla's and actually connects to a real-life story of being supported by the kind of Magneto(s) we are writing about here. These personal stories have no exact beginning, but for the sake of this chapter, we will locate it in Zach's story.

It began when some teachers and schools wanted to drug and kick Zach out of mainstream spaces for his difference, which is autism—despite the school system wanting to label his behavior as ADHD. Instead of complying, we sought out radical and alternative spaces, for both education and community, finding communities where folks were trying to think about how kids can be fully part of a community in liberated and autonomous ways. The key word here is *radical* because broadly speaking, in the youth liberation movement,

---

1   Marvel.com, "X-Men Comics," https://www.marvel.com/comics/characters/1009726/x-men.

there are many permutations of ways that adults work to create better spaces for (or with) youth to exercise their autonomy and power.

Many of these alternative schools and spaces are more in the realm of reform or emancipation, rather than full liberation from adult supremacy, while others go deeper into creating ways for youth to truly run and author their day-to-day lives. These reformist options can take shape in the creation of whole-school democratic meetings, having a say in which classes the kids get to take, and so on. When these projects or alternative schools are cut off from community and not embedded in larger movements for social change, they can seed an individualism, which actually isolates the individual child away from community, centering their penchants and desires in often selfish, cut off ways. This, of course, can have, and often does have, disastrous outcomes in a neoliberal, hyper-individualistic world. Which, of course, has very little to do with liberation, and side-steps justice, or entrenches other injustices. The X-Men story would fall more in the reform bracket of youth liberation movements.

Professor X did a lot of good for the mutant kids who were terrorized and kicked out of society; most notably, he founded a boarding school where younger mutants could learn from older mutant teachers. Don't get us wrong, he was vital to their survival, just as many adult allies are in real life. He even trusted them a lot, which was empowering to witness. However we are more interested in the messiness of finding ways to thrive amidst our differences, and a kind of collective thriving that requires a lot more trust and solidarity. Even though Professor X was known for saying the mutants weren't broken, and that they didn't need to be fixed, in the end, he was still working to assimilate them into society through traditional education and military training, despite the facade of liberation, justice, and thriving. For those of us who were either misfits or "bad" kids, we know how lifesaving a Professor X is, and how there are many of these kinds of adult allies within and outside mainstream institutions. They often provide a safe(r) space, in the form of their classroom, alternative school or after-school workshop, where your weirdness is accepted and even admired. But sometimes when you're hurting, you just need a break. You don't need to dash off to classes or join an army. We will circle back to this a bit later.

Magneto has, of course, always been at the whim of the writer. From his creation by Stan Lee, to Chris Claremont, and up to the most recent permutations, his story shifted and morphed through time, from a wounded anti-hero, to villain, to the ultimate hero (yet always colored with a sense of resentment) of the misfits. Throughout all of these storyline pivots, we think there are a few significant points to pull from his core character arc that speak to and support our argument of why he is a better example of supporting youth liberation and autonomy than Professor X, and the other X-Men.

The Magneto we see tends to be placed in a position of *ressentiment* and negation throughout the history of X-Men comics. His positionality is always framed from a place of negation as opposed to affirmation.[2] This framing results in the undermining of his potential throughout the various runs of the comic series (and other mediums). Framing Magneto as an angry, unthinking, reactionary is ideal for bringing attention away from the potentiality of his character, thus making Xavier look like the more "logical" and "ideal" figure for the mutants. The issues that arise from this dichotomy are numerous. In Stan Lee's own words, he "did not think of Magneto as a bad guy. He just wanted to strike back at the people who were so bigoted and racist … he was trying to defend the mutants, and because society was not treating them fairly he was going to teach society a lesson. He was a danger of course … but [I] never thought of him as a villain."[3] What's key here is that though he wasn't a villain, Lee himself saw the character's actions as based on misguided and dangerous methods. Probably most striking is the underlying fetishization of obedience and assimilation that runs very deep in this method of storytelling. Even in the cases where Magneto has been presented as the tragic romantic, an anti-hero who you really appreciate, his

2   Throughout the essay, we are using Nietzsche's ideas of *ressentiment*, etc., based primarily off Gilles Deleuze's work in *Nietzsche and Philosophy*, originally published in France in 1962.

3   Stan Lee, *Marvel Spotlight: Uncanny X-Men, 500 Issues Celebration* (New York: Marvel, 2008).

methods are almost always seen as morally reprehensible even when his actions "punching up" resemble nothing different from an average revolutionary act. The propaganda implicit here is quite obvious. To use the ever-present and over-discussed parallelism of Xavier as a Martin Luther King Jr. figure, and Magneto as a Malcolm X figure, we still see an uncomfortable rewriting of the actual work these revolutionary men contributed to their struggles. Xavier isn't the comic book equivalent of King, but instead the comic book equivalent of the "I Have a Dream" speech as interpreted by the dominating class. Even though King so famously wrote a scathing and powerful letter addressing "The White Moderate" in his open letter, "Letter from a Birmingham Jail,"[4] this very moderate approach painfully was and continues to be reproduced by the writers of X-Men. The propaganda runs deep.

Healing trauma and celebrating difference

"One must still have chaos in oneself to be able to give birth to a
dancing star."
—Friedrich Nietzsche, *Thus Spoke Zarathustra*

We understand where the message Professor X passed on to new kids comes from. Yet the frequently uttered message "you are not broken" is more often than not an erasure of trauma. In some sense, due to their trauma, they're all a bit broken, like most of us. Imagine if you had the mutation that Rogue (one of the X-Men) had, and every time you touched someone, they died! You would be pretty messed up by this, not just because humans (even other mutants) fear you, but because it's isolating and terrifying. But instead of finding ways for you to heal, let's get you decorated in pseudo-military gear, so you can be part of the X-Men, whose mission is to help keep safe the very empire that despises you. Of course, the boarding school and the X-Men did create a community for the mutants who had been abandoned by their families, due to their alienating powers, but to what end? At the base, it mimicked a typical private boarding school, steeped in competition, and then added militarism to the design. It's starting to not look like liberation to us.

With Xavier, you end up with the state apparatus masquerading as the kind father figure who "finally understands your alienation." It's important to keep in mind how this facade of so-called understanding (which often turns into

---

4   Martin Luther King Jr., "Letter from a Birmingham Jail," August 1963.

placating, and at its worst, gaslighting) is the very tool the state apparatus uses to capture and stratify the very people who have been alienated. The state itself understands that it's better to turn the alienated into tools you can carefully control, than to let them run free and potentially become dissidents and revolutionaries. Magneto supports dissidents and gives them space to exist freely outside the stratification of the state, prefiguring a liberated now.

Probably connected to the times in which it was created, in the world of X-Men, parents are assumed to be unable to accept the differences among their mutant children, and these mutants are only saved through the hand of a non-parental other, and the state-like institutions they are part of. This assumes that a parental figure can never truly come to understand the differences among their children and that what the kids need instead is to be warehoused in some kind of "alternative" institution, one that supports the colonial state, so they can be molded and turned into good citizens.[5]

How does this relate to our worlds? We think that "mutants" can be read not only as a metaphor for the alienating feeling of being young in an adult world, but also as a metaphor for neurodivergence and madness. The number of people—of all ages—who are being diagnosed and self-diagnosing as neurodivergent has proliferated in the last two decades. We see part of this breaking open of differences as correlating to the immense degree of hyperstimulation, global catastrophe, and isolation that has escalated in the last twenty years. We aren't necessarily saying that this correlation is evolutionary, but that, for many reasons, we are now seeing that more and more people have been revealed to be on the margins of contemporary society than before. To us, it is also the result of years of activists breaking down barriers, our increased access to information, and the dissemination of personal stories. As well, it's often easier to place blame on the individual for not fitting in (to school, etc.) due to their differences, rather than critique schools and other intuitions as the places that are not working. For this essay, we're interested in talking about "mutants" in the contemporary context: those who have started to transform away from/shed the veils and masks of the oppressive environments in which they and their recent ancestors have lived.

If you want to be an adult who supports kids, maybe in your kids' differences you will need a symbolic version of the helmet Magneto wears. This helmet could aid the parent (or adult) who wants to embrace kids' differences with delight and joy, and wearing a symbolic helmet will help ward off the rhetoric of the state and institutions that want to subdue, re/form, drug, and in some

---

5   We have also heard that the Matt Nix television show *The Gifted* challenges this idea.

cases hide them away. It doesn't matter how radical you are as a parent or adult friend, this helmet will be needed until we are in a different world. The original story of X-Men was reacting to and speaking for youth in the 1960s, and some of the newer renditions try to capture the current times, but in the end, the stories continue to affirm that these mutant youth continue to be misunderstood and thrown away, and the "moderate good guy" can protect them. Moreover, in these ongoing narratives, we think the story continues to fail in expressing the potentiality of Magneto as a beacon for finding belonging and youth autonomy.

It's by design

"There is no other world. There's just another way to live."
—Jacques Mesrine[6]

Comics can connect to us when we feel deeply alone and alienated. Especially as young people. But, they're also part of a rigged system—or the writers are—by which we mean that they write from their own biases and predilections. Of course they are brilliant in creating imagined characters and circumstances that may go beyond their lived experiences, but, like all writers, a part of them is in all they create.

As for the name "X-Men," the original writers, and for many decades, were cismen, and hence the name itself is enshrined in that hierarchy of patriarchy. Certainly, there are many writers who go beyond the limitations of patriarchy, but the gatekeepers at Marvel keep them out. It's no surprise then, that the writers of X-Men (even groundbreaking ones like Stan Lee) were limited in their scope, because we are up against centuries of crushing forces that fight to keep the status quo and the hierarchies in place.

These forces that subjugate and attempt to destroy our ways of relating are, and always were, designed to cut us off from our power, to stop us from revolting, and keep us from thriving. Silvia Federici's important work on the history of the witch trials is a way to see these developments at play.[7] She traces how capitalism developed a set of oppressive divisions as a strategy to sow distrust in communities. According to Federici, medieval Europe was nearing revolution and the state introduced witch trials as a way to interrupt and destroy these movements. They divided communities and sowed the seeds of distrust,

---

6   Quoted in The Invisible Committee, *To Our Friends* (Los Angeles: Semiotext(e), 2014).

7   Silvia Federici, *Caliban and the Witch* (New York: Autonomedia, 1998), 186, 188.

causing relationships to crumble. One of the stories often omitted from the history of the witch trials was that young girls, especially the daughters of the "witches," were also killed.[8]

Federici illustrates one of the most striking examples of a community pushing back when she tells of a community-wide resistance to the witch trials in a Basque fishing village (in the region of the Labourd). According to Federici the village had deeply rooted social bonds because the women ran the community during fishing seasons, so they were vital to its survival. When the priests came to start the witch trials, the community banded together to kick them out.[9] There's a lesson here about shared responsibility and deep bonds! As unrest continued to grow across Europe, the ruling class became more strategic in their pushback. During this time, the rise of charities happened to ward off systems of solidarity and mutual aid. And, alongside these institutions, of course, the rise of state and capital run institutions, such as orphanages and schools, to warehouse kids began to rise in most cities. It's also important to note that alongside the rise of all these institutions of control, there was always beautiful resistance, always a Magneto.

Destiny is autonomy

"I am Magneto and I have come to offer you sanctuary."
—Magneto

"I don't think that scale is our friend, it's our enemy. How to get together on small scale with patience, ethical regard for one another… maybe this renewal of our habits of assembly happens on a small scale."
—Fred Moten[10]

---

8   Ibid., 189.

9   Ibid.

10   Fred Moten in conversation with Robin D. G. Kelley, public lecture, University of Toronto, April 3, 2017.

Our Magneto moves beyond the limited scope in the comics and comes from a place of true affirmation, as opposed to resignation, negation, and *ressentiment*. Through his prefigurative community, he carves out a line of flight[11] from the mutant/human dichotomy, creating *with* his community a thriving autonomous zone that includes learning centers, health care spaces, gardens, and housing. Through affirming the multiplicity of experiences among mutants, and giving them a space to be true to themselves, he joins together with them to affirm their own existence, engage in mutual aid, and share their collective power. Alongside the everyday work of living and fighting to crush injustices, they can find ways to heal and embrace joy.

This Magneto is more interested in *hearing from* the mutants themselves—including the very young—about what they need. And through this deep listening, together they slowly build what they need, creating a web of many autonomy zones—not just one large alternative State. Because centralizing a large movement comes with all the problems inherent in emulation of the very structure you are fighting. To truly deconstruct the systems we are fighting, we will have to keep wearing our helmets to ward off their pervasive rhetoric, especially those by folks claiming to be for the same justices. In doing this, together we will find productive ways to dislodge ourselves from the symbolic structures of Empire.

Because each autonomy zone will continue to be under attack by the State, there will always be a need for systems of communications and strategies, a kind of verticalism that will connect each horizontally run autonomous zone to ensure the survival of all. Part of this will require weapons, too, just like in

---

11   Félix Guattari and Gilles Deleuze, *Anti-Oedipus: Capitalism and Schizophrenia* (Minneapolis: University of Minnesota Press, 1972).

the comics (Magneto's army). The armed part of the resistance is of course small compared to the creation of learning centers, healthcare spaces, gardens and farms to grow their own food—all the subtle and concrete ways to create a rich community resilience that is rooted in self-determination and autonomy.

—And play! Kids are everywhere, too, similar to this quote in *The Dispossessed*, where Ursula K. Le Guin writes: "Children were around, some involved in the work with the adults, some underfoot making mud pies, some busy with games in the street, one sitting perched up on the roof of the learning center with her nose deep in a book."[12]

With our version of the figure Magneto, we see it is vitally important that all the autonomy zones be multigenerational and based on a coming together across differences, a beautiful web of relationships based on a foundation of trust and responsibility. Together, this all-ages, vastly different group of folks will create a vibrant community and keep it going; everyone will have a role in making it work. It will be a vibrant place where the helmets are eventually taken off, to instead be used to grow flowers.

There are many Magnetos in our communities… You may even be one. It's something that can happen at any age. At age seven, Zach was one for carla, and vice versa. carla trusted Zach when he wasn't thriving at school and was wanting something else. Magnetos are often demonized through media and other propaganda as violent and dangerous. But to us, the Magneto we painted above is the ultimate accomplice for youth liberation and autonomy, someone (you?) who works with others to unbuild walls and co-create worlds where children and youth are free to be their full selves, to heal, and to be an active member in their communities. This is love.

---

12   Ursula K. Le Guin, *The Dispossessed* (New York: Harper Perennial, 2014), 99.

Back to the Beginning / Outro

youth ellipsis: an ode to echolalia
By kitty sipple

(the you is I and the me is we because all time is happening at all times so we
    are kids and you are me)

trust kids. trust kids too.
trust kids to know.
trust kids to know no so when you hear their no you know they know their no.
trust kids to know themselves before they know you / kids will author their
own stories before they invite you to read them / kids will invite you to know
them only when they trust you to know your own stories / kids will know you
before you know yourself / kids will know that magneto was right / kids know.

trust kids.
trust kids too.
trust kids   to be.
                    to be kids.
trust kids   to be kids who know themselves in a language that you have
never spoken / to create languages that you may learn to speak if you learn to
listen / to speak the stories that they know in ways that they may never know
/ to create the new worlds in which they want to live in / to grow in the ways
that they want to be rooted / to live in their truth before you even begin to
understand them as a human in the multiverse.
trust kids   to be kids in a world that does not want them to be kids.
trust kids   to be kids.

> to be   neurodivergent.
>   neuroemergent.
>   neurodifferent.
>   neurofabulous.
>   neurodimensional.
>   neuroqueer.

trust kids   to be.

trust (these) kids.
trust (those) kids too.
trust kids / all kids / sad kids / mad kids / happy kids / Black kids / Indigenous kids / magical kids / anxious kids / quiet kids / outspoken kids / undocumented kids / adopted kids / thoughtful kids / tree-climbing kids / naming-all-the-frogs-George kids / otherworld otherworld-daydreaming kids / mutain'eering kids / screaming kids / joyful kids / disabled kids / grieving kids / autistic kids / sick kids / scared kids / hurt kids / traumatized kids / non-verbal kids / compassionate kids / empathetic kids / system kids / hypervigilant kids / voice-hearing kids / stimming kids / hungry kids / tired kids / ticcing kids / hopeful kids / trans kids / queer kids / intersex kids / 2SLGBTQIAA+ kids / all (and we mean all) kids. because this list is not exhaustive of kids to trust
how about
just
trust (all) kids.

trust kids because it is quite possible that you were not trusted as a kid / you know how it feels to not be trusted / it hurts to be not trusted when you were a kid / it hurts to be not trusted when you are a kid
and that is not okay.
        that is not okay.
        that mistrust is not okay.
        that mistrust of kids is not okay.
        that mistrust of kids while you were a kid is not okay.
        that mistrust of kids has now been passed on to you as an adult
            & the remedy to this is simple
            & requires you to simply
trust kids.

trust (all) kids because all kids deserve to be.

trust (all) kids because all kids deserve to be trusted / you deserve to have been trusted / your kids deserve to be trusted / my kids deserve to be trusted / our kids deserve to be trusted / all kids deserve to be trusted.

trust kids.

trust kids to not want what you want.

trust kids to not want what you want to give them / to gift them / to pass on to them / to sell to them / to coerce on them / to force on them / to advertise to them / to add to them.

trust kids to say.
trust kids to say no.
trust kids to say their no.

trust kids to say no racial violence / colonized violence / capitalistic violence / patriarchal violence / gender violence / sexual violence / housing instability / food insecurity / assigned gender you forced on them at birth / to the name you gave them before you knew them / to the food you thought they liked before you asked them / to their picture posted everywhere without consent / hegemonic systems / cops / prisons / pathologized psychiatric violence / to your government / to your politics / to your history / to your empire / to any of your violence

trust kids because you have been taught
    you have embodied
    you have been taught to not trust kids.
    you have been taught to not trust kids
        as the (tiny) humans they are
        as the (youthful) humans they are as the kids they are
        because kids who are kids are not to be trusted so kids
        should not be kids.

when does that happen?
(all time is happening always)

where are kids no longer kids?
(space time is non-linear)

why are kids stolen from being kids?
(*this is not about being an adult*)

how do kids stop being kids?
(*this is about agency & autonomy at any age*)

the answer: because (*somewhere/somehow*) adults stopped trusting kids.
                                 adults stopped trusting kids.
                                 (old kids) stopped trusting (young) kids.

this is a statement a fact an unknown known truth and yet
there was never a question and yet
the answer

is always
always
trust kids.

"Why struggle to open a door between us when the whole wall is an illusion?"
—Rumi

Bios

(in order of appearance)

carla joy bergman (she/they) currently lives in Vancouver, British Columbia, on the lands of the xʷməθkʷəym (Musqueam), Skwxwú7mesh (Squamish), and Selíĺwitulh (Tsleil-Waututh) Nations, with her kids and partner. They are a mom, a deprofessional weaver, writer, and neuro-emergent. carla has spent the past two decades working with community to create collaborative multi-media platforms that range from print to films. carla loves to zoom in on the in-between happenings and issues and bust binaries. She is the coauthor of *Joyful Militancy*, AK Press/IAS 2017; editor of the book, *Radiant Voices*, TouchWood Ed, 2019; co-founder of the podcast platform, *Grounded Futures*; and is currently working on a couple of books. In January 2022, carla and her partner Chris launched a pamphlet series called, *lowercase* at Listening House Media.

Matt Hern lives on the middle arm of the Fraser River in xʷməθkʷəy̓əm (Musqueam) territory. He is the co-founder and co-director of Solid State Community Industries.

The Curiousism Cyphers is an anonymous writers' collective, bickering about the concept of time, justice, and autonomy. They remain anonymous to implode the cult of personality and individuality that often overshadows ideas and stories. Reach out to them at: CuriousismCyphers@protonmail.com.

Chris Bergman is a producer, editor, artist, technician, and photographer. He is currently collaborating on a few sound design projects with and for community, and is illustrating and writing a children's book. Chris lives and works in Vancouver, on the lands of the xʷməθkʷəym (Musqueam),

Skwxwú7mesh (Squamish), and Selílwitulh (Tsleil-Waututh) Nations, with his kids and partner.

ck nosun lives in Kingston/Katarokwi, where they make digital works intended to promote anti-authoritarian, anti-colonial, and anti-capitalist struggles.

Noleca Radway is the founder of Quarks, a family production company specializing in audio and visual art though a Black queer lens. Noleca is a producer, emergent strategist, educator, speaker, writer, screenwriter, host, and director. She is the producer and host of the progressive parenting podcast *Raising Rebels*. She is also the former executive director of the Brooklyn Free School. Noleca recently served as Impact Producer for POV/American Documentary's *Otherly* series, producing educational resources and panel discussions. She also produced HBO's *Between the World and Me* podcast, highlighting her unique ability to amplify multiple voices and mediums to tell a story and create impact. She considers the ability to make connections between people, philosophies, and dimensions her personal superpower. She attributes this to being a Bronx-raised, first- generation Black-Jamaican wife, mother, teacher, educator, and Octavia Butler fan. Noleca graduated from Howard University and attended Bank Street College of Education. She lives in Amsterdam with her partner and their three kids.

Dani Burlison (she/her) is a writer, teacher, and witch living in Sonoma County, California, with her cats, chickens, and houseplants. She is the editor of *All of Me: Love, Anger, and the Female Body* (PM Press), the author of *Some Places Worth Leaving* (Tolsun Books) and *Dendrophilia and Other Social Taboos*, a collection of essays based on her McSweeney's Internet Tendency column of the same name. Her articles, essays, and short stories can be found online and in several print publications. You can find out more at www.daniburlison.com.

Enfys Craft (he/him/they/them) is a trans-masculine nonbinary witch and astrologer who lives in Northern California with plants. He loves plant propagation, cats, jewelry, and lavender soda.

Uilliam (Liam) Joy Bergman spends most of his time with their friends and family, talking, sharing, making food, and talking about surviving capitalism. He is grateful to have felt trusted all his life, and is an unschooler/life learner. Liam is the co-host of the podcast, the *Grounded Futures Show*. At seventeen, he feels cautiously hopeful for the future. Liam uses he/they/it pronouns.

Yasamin Holland is an artist and educator based out of Brunswick, Maine.

Tim Holland (aka Sole) is a rapper, activist, and permaculturist based out of Brunswick, Maine.

chris time steele is a co-learner, hip-hop artist, journalist, storyteller, and writer. steele has an MA and is a precarious teacher who seeks to work outside typical pedagogy, experimenting with hip-hop and co-mentorship. steele contributes to Truthout, has co-authored works with Noam Chomsky, and is host of the *Time Talks* podcast. Through music, under the alias Time, steele has worked with Common, Mick Jenkins, Xiu Xiu, and Psalm One.

Idzie Desmarais is a grown unschooler who has been living, thinking, and writing about self-directed education for most of her life. Her writing is deeply informed by her anarchistic politics, her experience of queerness and chronic illness. She is a sporadic but enthusiastic reader of novels and nonfiction alike, and sees her writing as a constant quest to untangle chaotic thoughts and forge connections with others through words. Idzie lives in the Montreal, Canada, but dreams of living in the woods.

JLG is a Squamish/Portuguese mother/artist who uses technology and storytelling to stimulate meaningful dialogue that challenges the status quo and encourages systemic change.

Akilah S. Richards is an author and digital content writer. Her liberation-focused work explores unconventional parenting and lifestyle choices to help people leave or change the environments where they do not feel free or safe as themselves. She is an intersectional feminist writer with a keen focus on amplifying the spectrum of Black and Brown voices in the self-directed education (unschooling) movement. Her book, *Raising Free People: Unschooling as Liberation and Healing Work,* came out on PM Press in 2020.

Meghan Carrico is an educational consultant, principal of a school, distributed learning teacher, partner, mother, and recently a grandmother. She works and lives out of Vancouver and Victoria. Her passion is helping people start schools, learning centers, home learning groups, and finding the right fit for their family. She has a BA from Antioch college, a teaching certificate from Simon Fraser University, and a MA from Royal Roads University. Her experience at Windsor House school as a child, teacher, mother, and principal led her on a path to support families in finding an educational environment that is right for them. She is currently interested in helping families build community and discover new and bold paths that support their child's learning

Antonio Buehler (he/him) founded Abrome to support the liberation of children and fundamentally change the way people think about education. He wants learners to have full autonomy over their bodies, minds, and time so they can lead meaningful and purposeful lives, positively impact society, and improve the human condition. Abrome is aligned with Antonio's desire to challenge, undermine, and create alternatives to oppressive systems so we can move toward a freer, healthier world. Antonio also founded the Peaceful Streets Project, which was one of the most active copwatch organizations in the United States from 2012 to 2017.

Sara Zacuto is a former preschool teacher and parent educator who specializes in the Reggio approach. She cares deeply about the rights of children, and wants to see the world become a place where children's voices and ideas are lifted up and respected. She loves writing, thrifting, and collecting books. She lives in Orange, California, with her husband Gabe, two children, and four cats.

Rebecca Solnit is writer, historian, and activist. She is the author of more than twenty books on feminism, western and urban history, popular power, social change, and insurrection, wandering and walking, hope and catastrophe. Her books include *Orwell's Roses; Recollections of My Nonexistence; Hope in the Dark; Men Explain Things to Me;* and *A Paradise Built in Hell: The Extraordinary Communities that Arise in Disaster.* A product of the California public education system from kindergarten to graduate school, she writes regularly for the *Guardian* and *Lithub* and serves on the board of the climate group Oil Change International.

Jon Pawson (Ngāti Porou/Pākehā) is an anarchist, ex-postal worker, and union organizer in Aotearoa, New Zealand. He drinks whiskey and eats tofu. He occasionally posts on Instagram about what he's been reading at @anarchistreadinglist.

Tasnim Nathoo is a social worker with an interest in unschooling, mental wellness, and healing justice. She lives in Vancouver, traditional territories of the xʷməθkʷəym (Musqueam), S̲k̲wx̲wú7mesh (Squamish), and Selíl̓witulh (Tsleil-Waututh) Nations. Visit her website to learn more about her work: www.tasnimnathoo.com.

Helen Hughes was born and raised in British Columbia. She started a free school for her daughter whose spirit was dying in regular school. Helen and the school grew up together during the next forty-five years. She is now a grandmother of four, a great-grandmother of one, the former matriarch of the school.

Maya Motoi is an unschooled, half "Japanese" half Dutch "Canadian" person, who is queer, an anarchist, and a feminist. (Impartial to pronouns.) Maya grew up in "Japan," spending their teen years in "Vancouver, British Columbia, Canada," located on the unceded territories of the Coast Salish, and has been living in "Japan" since 2013. When in "Vancouver," Maya was involved at the Purple Thistle Centre. These days Maya spends most of her time entangling their time with others, in what might be known as "care" or "support" in a few different forms. Basically, all of this is about cultivating relationships in all the clumsy messy ways that we do. These things are framed within and are a part of the threads woven together by people and movements that fought for disability justice and women's rights.

Wakaba Mine was born in 1971 and grew up in Iizuka, Fukuoka, within a family typical of the economic growth period: father had a monthly salary maintaining home and car ownership and two kids, mother started to work a little after having the kids... Wakaba has dealt with addiction due to things including being sexually abused within their extended family when young and the mother/daughter relationship they had. Wakaba believes that the internal oppression they experience is rooted in things such as patriarchy and war, furthermore, the problems of colonialism, authority, and private property. Currently they are interested in the folk culture of the Chikuho area (a coal mining area) where they grew up, as well as how it was for "women" to have lived in this area.

Joanna Motoi grew up in Ottawa, Ontario. She did East Asian studies along with English and Film studies at the University of Toronto. She has now lived in Japan for over thirty years and continues her study in East Asian philosophy independently. For most of those thirty years, she has been teaching English to children, and through this started to research extensively about education and our relationships with children. She enjoys country life in an old Japanese farmhouse with three cats and a partner who excels at self-learning.

Cindy White is an eighteen-year-old Latina Jewish non-binary being who is quiet when first meeting people and opens up closely as you get to know her. In addition to being an artist, she is a time traveler and a lucid dreamer with microcephaly and learning disabilities. Cindy wishes for all people to have safe spaces for their voices to be heard.

kitty sipple is a thirty-nine-year-old white disabled queer femme trans non-binary person. They are Mad, autistic, and multiple. kitty is interested in Mad liberation, grief care work, and reclamation of extreme states. They currently live on the land of the Dakota and Ojibwe, in the city otherwise known as Minneapolis.

Chris Mercogliano worked with children for thirty-five years at the Albany Free School, the oldest inner-city alternative school in the United States. He is the author of *Making It Up As We Go Along, the Story of the Albany Free School* (Heinemann 1998); *Teaching the Restless: One School's Remarkable No-Ritalin Approach to Helping Children Learn and Succeed* (Beacon Press 2004); *How to Grow a School: Starting and Sustaining Schools That Work* (Oxford Village Press

2006); and *In Defense of Childhood: Protecting Kids' Inner Wildness* (Beacon Press 2007). His essays, commentaries, and reviews have appeared in newspapers, magazines, and journals around the world, as well as in seven anthologies; and he has been featured on National Public Radio's *All Things Considered*, Canadian Broadcasting Corporation Radio's *Ideas*, and many other nationally syndicated radio shows. The father of two wonderful daughters, he lives with his wife Betsy on a one-acre farm in downtown Albany, New York.

Lily Mercogliano Easton is an educator who lives with her three kids and husband in Albany, New York most of the year and in Southfield, Massachusetts, in the summer, where she is the camp director of Camp WA WA Segowea. Before she became a camp director, Lily grew up at the Free School in Albany, attended public high school, graduated from Northeastern University as a certified teacher, and then went on to teach and become head of school for twelve years at Brooklyn Free School.

Toby Rollo, PhD is a professor of political science at Lakehead University, who specializes in political theory and Canadian politics.

Dr. Stacey Patton is a child abuse survivor and former foster youth turned award-winning journalist, college professor, and child advocate. Her writings on race, education, and child welfare issues have appeared in the *New York Times, Washington Post, Al Jazeera*, and many other outlets. She is the author of *That Mean Old Yesterday; Spare the Kids: Why Whupping Children Won't Save Black America*; and the forthcoming *Strung Up: The Lynching of Black Children in Jim Crow America*. She is also the creator of www.sparethekids.com.

Gustavo Esteva (August 20, 1936– March 17, 2022) is a DE professionalized intellectual and nomadic storyteller. He assumed that he was an activist for the last fifty years, until he discovered that he was activated by the people at the grassroots with whom he was living and working, mainly Indigenous people. He has been very close to the Zapatistas and Zapatismo. He lived in a small Zapotec village, in Oaxaca, Mexico.

Madhu Suri Prakash's politics of hope has its deep roots in the soil of friendship-festing. Her cherished conspirators include those transforming lawnscapes into Victory/friendship garden growing communities—offering nourishing, bountiful harvests of fruits, flowers, and vegetables to creatures small and large.

Dana L. Stuchul was once an apostle of and is now apostate from education-cum-schooling. She seeks in her efforts in her neighborhood, in her own living/being, and within Penn State's College of Education, to re-envision and transform hierarchies and related ideas (epistemic, ontologic, institutional, et al.) in service to worlds made more peaceable, just, and beautiful.

Gabriel Zacuto is an Artist, Writer, Partner, Parent, and Antiauthoritarian Leftist Surviving in Southern California.

Zach Bergman is an artist, writer, record label owner, and a composer. He holds a MA in electro-acoustics and composition from the University of Birmingham, UK. You can find Zach's music under the moniker Sour Gout and Collapsed Structures.

Grant Hoskins, aka Gadzooks Bazooka is a self-taught artist who has been creating art from since childhood. His art can be found locally and internationally in galleries, zines, music album covers, and pieces in the streets of Southern California.

AK PRESS is small, in terms of staff and resources, but we also manage to be one of the world's most productive anarchist publishing houses. We publish close to twenty books every year, and distribute thousands of other titles published by like-minded independent presses and projects from around the globe. We're entirely worker run and democratically managed. We operate without a corporate structure—no boss, no managers, no bullshit.

The **FRIENDS OF AK PRESS** program is a way you can directly contribute to the continued existence of AK Press, and ensure that we're able to keep publishing books like this one! Friends pay $25 a month directly into our publishing account ($30 for Canada, $35 for international), and receive a copy of every book AK Press publishes for the duration of their membership! Friends also receive a discount on anything they order from our website or buy at a table: 50% on AK titles, and 30% on everything else. We have a Friends of AK ebook program as well: $15 a month gets you an electronic copy of every book we publish for the duration of your membership. *You can even sponsor a very discounted membership for someone in prison.*

Email **friendsofak@akpress.org** for more info, or visit the website: **https://www.akpress.org/friends.html**.

There are always great book projects in the works—so sign up now to become a Friend of AK Press, and let the presses roll!